WYNKEN·BLYNKEN
AND·NOD·ONE·NIGHT·
SAILED·OFF·IN·A
WOODEN·SHOE·
SAILED·ON·A·RIVER·OF
CRYSTAL·LIGHT
INTO·A·SEA·OF·DEW·
WHERE·ARE·YOU·GOING
AND·WHAT·DO·YOU·WISH·
THE·OLD·MOON·
ASKED·THE·THREE·
WE·HAVE·COME·TO·FISH
FOR·THE·HERRING·FISH
THAT·LIVE·IN·THIS·
BEAUTIFUL··SEA·
NETS·OF·SILVER·AND
GOLD·HAVE·WE·SAID.

D1228783

Field Days

From Eugene Field's ❧ AN AUTO-ANALYSIS

I dislike "Politics," so called.

I should like to have the privilege of voting extended to women.

I am unalterably opposed to capital punishment.

I favor a system of pensions for noble services in literature, art, science, etc. I approve of compulsory education.

If I had my way, I should make the abuse of horses, dogs, and cattle a penal offense; I should abolish all dog laws and dog-catchers, and I would punish severely everybody who caught and caged birds.

I dislike all exercise and play all games very indifferently.

I love to read in bed.

I believe in churches and schools: I hate wars, armies, soldiers, guns, and fireworks.

I like music (limited).

I have been a great theater-goer.

I enjoy the society of doctors and clergymen.

My favorite color is red.

I do not care particularly for sculpture or for paintings; I try not to become interested in them, for the reason that if I were to cultivate a taste for them I should presently become hopelessly bankrupt.

I am extravagantly fond of perfumes.

I am a poor diner, and I drink no wine or spirits of any kind: I do not smoke tobacco.

I dislike crowds and I abominate functions.

I am six feet in height; am of spare build, weigh 160 pounds, and have shocking taste in dress.

But I like to have well-dressed people about me.

My eyes are blue, my complexion pale, my face is shaven, and I incline to baldness.

It is only when I look and see how young and fair and sweet my wife is that I have a good opinion of myself.

I am fond of the companionship of women, and I have no unconquerable prejudice against feminine beauty. I recall with pride that in twenty-two years of active journalism I have always written in reverential praise of womankind.

I favor early marriage.

I do not love all children.

I have tried to analyze my feelings toward children, and I think I discover that I love them in so far as I can make pets of them.

I believe that, if I live, I shall do my best literary work when I am a grandfather.

Denver Public Library

FIELD

Field Days

The Life, Times, & Reputation of Eugene Field

by

ROBERT CONROW

❧❧

Charles Scribner's Sons
New York

Copyright © 1974 Robert Conrow

Library of Congress Cataloging in Publication Data

Conrow, Robert.
  Field days.

  Bibliography: p.
  1. Field, Eugene, 1850–1895——Biography.   I. Title.
PS1668.C6   811′.4 [B]   73–19358
ISBN   0—684—13780—1

This book published simultaneously in the
United States of America and in Canada—
Copyright under the Berne Convention

All rights reserved. No part of this book
may be reproduced in any form without the
permission of Charles Scribner's Sons.

1 3 5 7 9 11 13 15 17 19 C/C 20 18 16 14 12 10 8 6 4 2

Printed in the United States of America

To Ginny who shared in living and growing and Aaron who joined in the process.

Acknowledgments

I would like to thank the following people at the University of Michigan who helped considerably in the initial stages of this work: Marvin Felheim, David Angus, Richard Latner, and Robert Sklar.

Most of all, I cannot give thanks enough to Russell Gregory whose good spirits and scholarly commentary saw this book through to completion.

Contents

Introduction

At a time when discontent and severe national doubt seemed pervasive on the American horizons, the eccentric personality of Eugene Field skipped, danced, and otherwise entertained the imaginations of thousands. Field's humorous "Sharps and Flats" column for the Chicago *Daily News* was faithfully read, his poems of childhood were eulogized and set to music, and, ultimately, his reputation so escalated in the twentieth century that even today there is scarcely a major midwestern city without a school, library, or park memorial named after the once-celebrated poet.

In resuscitating his memory, I have denied all impulses to speculate about the nature of the inner man. This would have been not only inappropriate, but virtually impossible: in Field's case there are few truly private papers accessible. Rather, I have sought to rediscover the basic impulses which drew men, women, and children together to partake in the spectacle of his remarkable performance. The reactions of his audience—whether naïve, senti-mental, or paradoxical—serve today as a keen barometer of the hopes and fantasies of past generations. As such, they indicate not so much what people actually believed, but, perhaps more impor-tantly, what they *wanted* to believe and what they tenaciously wanted to avoid.

Because of the time and the atmosphere, Field was offered and willingly accepted a protective garb of respectability—a garb which was wonderfully fitted and impeccably maintained by well-meaning friends and biographers. That Field himself once referred to his nursery rhymes as "mother rot" and was widely known amongst his male friends as a facile bard of bawdy verse seemed unimportant to his loyal preservationists. Rather, it was the ideal which seemed worthy of their tireless efforts.

Photographs have been selected to provide the reader with a first-hand glimpse of those forces which so strongly determined the nature of Field's presence in the public mind. Because documenta-tion has been preferred to mere illustration, I have often picked the amateur's photograph before that of the professional.

Because I have focused on the dialogue which existed between the poet-journalist and his audience, it now seems important to recount, in briefest fashion, those events which formed the basis of Field's journalistic success.

❧ INTRODUCTION ❧

September 2, 1850	Eugene Field was born in St. Louis to Frances and Roswell M. Field.
1857–1869	After the death of his mother in 1856, Eugene was sent East to live under the custody of his cousin, Mary Field French. He attended schools in Monson and Williamstown, Massachusetts.
1869–1871	In 1869, Field enrolled at Knox College in Galesburg, Illinois where his guardian, John W. Burgess, was on the faculty. He later joined his younger brother, Roswell, at the University of Missouri.
1872–1873	Upon receiving his inheritance, Field embarked for a Grand Tour of the British Isles and western Europe.
October 16, 1873	Field married Julia Sutherland Comstock who, during the next several years, gave birth to eight children, five of whom lived past childhood.
1873–1883	Field worked on the following newspapers: St. Louis *Journal* (1873–1875) ; St. Joseph *Gazette* (1875–1876) ; St. Louis *Times-Journal* (1876–1880) ; Kansas City *Times* (1880–1881) ; Denver *Tribune* (1881–1883).
1883–1895	In 1883, Field moved to Chicago to begin writing his "Sharps and Flats" column for the morning edition of the Chicago *Daily News.* Although the *Morning News* was known as the *Chicago Record* after 1893, it remained a part

of the *Daily News* operation. During this time, Field wrote several published volumes of satire, prose, and poetry. No doubt his best remembered poems today are "Wynken, Blynken and Nod" and "The Duel" (otherwise known as "The Gingham Dog and the Calico Cat"). In terms of the building of his reputation, however, his most significant poem was "Little Boy Blue."

Little Boy Blue.

The little toy dog is covered with dust
But sturdy and staunch he stands,
And the little toy soldier is red with rust
And his musket moulds in his hands.
Time was when the little toy dog was new
And the soldier was passing fair,
And that was the time when our Little Boy Blue
Kissed them and put them there.

"Now don't you go 'til I come", he said,
"And don't you make any noise!"
So, toddling off to his trundle bed,
He dreamt of the pretty toys.
And as he was dreaming, an angel song
Awakened our Little Boy Blue —
Oh, the years are many – the years are long –
But the little toy friends are true!

Aye, faithful to Little Boy Blue, they stand –
Each in the same old place,
Awaiting the touch of a little hand,
The smile of a little face.
And they wonder — as waiting these long years through
In the dust of that little chair –
What has become of
That they never have seen our Little Boy Blue
Since he kissed them and put them there.

#

The Scene
at His Death

For thirty years the house had remained unchanged. In 1895, the den had been described as "the most wonderful room in all the city." In the words of one reporter, it was a long, high room, covered with "a thousand and one relics that the poet had picked up in various parts of the world. And it is cluttered up with heaps of his favourite books and hung with ancient pictures and photographs." Another visitor to this same room in 1895 had been similarly impressed. "There never was such a library before, and it is not likely there ever will be again. There is a Canton flannel elephant with a scarlet and gold howdah on top of one bookcase, flanked by old glass and things Etruscan." Mechanical toys, including a black bear with snapping jaws and a dancing harlequin, competed for the visitor's attention with strange pewter dishes, old blue china as delicate and fragile as a cobweb, and a huge wall-to-wall bookcase containing one of the most complete collections of Horace in the world.

For thirty years, in accordance with the wishes of the poet's wife, the house had remained unchanged. Then, in 1925, at Christmastime, came word that "the little toy dog must desert his post. The little toy soldier has marching orders. The gingham dog and calico cat are dispossessed. The sugar-plum tree is uprooted. Wynken, Blynken and Nod are homeless."

Eugene Field's home in Chicago was to be sacrificed for the sake of an eight-story apartment building. Despite considerable protest, the demolition experts began their work before New Year's Day, 1926. J. A. Culden, to take one example, had written a letter to the New York *Evening World* asking if there was not one man who might come forward to save the house. "There are a half a dozen 'schools of the new literature,' " noted Mr. Culden, "now turning out blank verse, labor propaganda and erotics by the ream. Who among them could stand in the shoes of Eugene Field?" Most had to admit there were few who could. Yet, ultimately, Field fans were forced to accept the verdict of the Louisville *Courier-Journal* columnist who lamented that "material progress hasn't the habit of stepping around obstacles."

Julia Field, her dreams for preservation of the Field house shattered, departed for her farm at Tomahawk, Wisconsin. An article in the Boston *Evening Transcript* noted that "the widow has kept only a pair of little Boy Blue's baby shoes and a toy horse." The renowned Field library of some 4,500 volumes was dispatched to New York, where it was put up for auction by the Anderson galleries.

Prior to the wreckers' arrival, a reporter for the Chicago *Daily*

News visited the Victorian dwelling, carefully noting his impressions:

> In the deserted hallway of the old home a bronze bust of Field looks on what is left. The bust seems to peer largely over all the front rooms—remembering, one can imagine, scenes of other days. And now it sees an old clock with broken hands, the peeling calcimined walls, fine old lamps empty of light bulbs, the rugless floors, and outside the great lawn—now given to the ministration of dandelion and ragweed.

Thirty years before, on the evening of November 3, 1895, Eugene Field, the "Children's Laureate," the writer of "Little Boy Blue," the familiar author of "Sharps and Flats" for the Chicago *Record,* had dimmed the fine old lamps for the last time. Beside him in bed, and not far from the writing table where Field recently had written the last chapter of *The Love Affairs of a Bibliomaniac,* slept Frederick, or "Daisy," as the father preferred to call his fourteen-year-old son. Packages, addressed but unmailed, rested on a corner of the table. One of them bore the name of General Nelson A. Miles and another that of the bookdealer George M. Millard.

At 4:30 that morning, though it seemed to him he had just fallen asleep, Daisy was awakened by his father's heavy breathing. Glancing over, he became frightened at the strange pallor of his father's face, then dropped back upon his pillow and remained silent some ten minutes. The breathing continued, punctuated by only the ticking of the clocks throughout the house. Near the bed was a clock with a gong in it like a country dinner-bell which clanged the hour with a loud metal ring; and close by was Field's "freak clock," as he called it, made entirely of wood, which ticked like a hammer striking hard wood.

A guest in the house, Mr. George Yenowine, awakened by Daisy, ran to Field's bedroom. "When I got there," noted Yenowine, "I found he was already dead. He was lying in an easy position and the expression on his face was that of a man sleeping. He could not have been dead many minutes, for his body was still quite warm."

Shortly, the sun would rise over Lake Michigan, peering in through the red curtains, glancing upon the red rugs, and finally resting upon the fantastic, swirl-patterned, red wallpaper. An article in *St. Nicholas* Magazine the following year would compare this room, with its "barbaric colors and effects," to the room Susan Bates furnished in Henry Blake Fuller's *With the Procession*. The article pointed out that Susan Bates had furnished her room "like the primitive one she had occupied when a girl in her father's house." The article then noted that "this was partly Eugene Field's idea in furnishing his own room. He was fond of grotesque effects, he loved red passionately, and he wanted a reminder of the furnishings of a century ago."

At first, news of the death spread in hushed tones through the large houses of the northern suburbs. Dr. Hodges and Dr. Hawley were summoned to the Field house about six o'clock, while Field's close friend Dr. Frank Reilly, the Assistant Commissioner of Health, arrived a short time later. All three doctors concurred that death had been caused by heart failure. Dr. Reilly then pronounced the death officially to have been caused by the formation of a clot of blood in the heart.

By coincidence, initial reports of the death were registered in Milwaukee. Mr. George Yenowine was editor of the Milwaukee

Illustrated News. Retaining his reporter's sensibilities even in this time of personal crisis, he telegraphed his paper. From there, the shocking item was put on the Associated Press wires and flashed across the country.

Melville E. Stone, managing editor of the Associated Press and Field's former boss on the Chicago *Daily News,* reached his downtown office just before 7:00 a.m. A messenger greeted him with a copy of the release from Wisconsin. Suspecting a hoax, Mr. Stone nonetheless left immediately for Field's home in suburban Buena Park.

Already, the neighborhood was beginning to stir with the dreadful tidings. An article in the Chicago *Tribune* the following morning would note: "The first arrivals were Mr. and Mrs. H. H. Kohlsaat at 7:30 o'clock, and the next were Mr. and Mrs. M. E. Stone. After these came the K. A. Waller family, Edward Winslow's family, John Hiltman's family, Hart Taylor's family, and so on until nearly all the people in Buena Park had called."

Within a few hours, word reached passersby in downtown Chicago. And by noon, every volume of any of his works in the large stock of McClurg & Co. in Chicago was sold and orders were flooding in for more. In answer to a reporter's query, George M. Millard—whose package lay unopened beside Field's bed—noted that "his books are selling all over America. His 'A Little Book of Western Verse' leads all other American books in sales excepting those of Gen. Lew Wallace. When I was in London this summer they were deeply interested in him over there."

For some, news of the death would come as an almost incomprehensible shock. "Eugene Field dead," cried Opie Read, "my God, this is terrible. What kind of a man was he? Well, you won't see his like again in a long time. He was one of the most striking men I ever knew. People would be drawn to him instinctively. He always had a doll for a little girl, and always had a story for the children and they all loved him as only children can love."

Hamlin Garland would not learn of the death of his friend until mid-afternoon, when he dropped in at Stone & Kimball's Publishing Company in the Caxton Building. Unable to speak for several minutes, Garland's voice faltered, his brow dropped and he finally uttered simply that he could not "bear to speak in a newspaper way at this time. I knew him intimately, loved him profoundly and admired him greatly as a man and as a writer."

That evening, newspapers throughout the city, state, and country registered the shock of a nation. Seldom, noted the Chicago *Tribune,* has the "death of a citizen of Chicago in a private station occasioned such sincere and universal sorrow. On the streets, in the marts of trade, and at the clubs, universal regret was expressed at the loss of such a genius by the thousands who have enjoyed his acquaintance, his writings, and his public readings."

Word came from New York that "all the evening papers contain long and sincere tributes to the late Eugene Field." The *Telegram* referred to Field as "the inimitable newspaper humorist and poet," while the New York *Mail and Express* perhaps best caught the sentiment of the country. "Chicago gave him a home," declared the writer for the *Mail and Express,* "but the nation long since gave him a chair at every fireside where his work is known. His verse could force a smile where a tear yet lingered in the eye." The New York *Times,* in a more sedate vein, reported that "in fifteen years Eugene Field had become as familiarly known as any writer of verse in this country, and he had made a circle of personal acquaintances and admirers almost as wide as his reputation."

1 ⚬ *The Scene at His Death*

From Washington, D.C., where the announcement of Field's death came as a shock to his congressional friends, to St. Joseph, Missouri, where the City Council resolved that "the good influence of his sweet song and pure literature will live so long as civilization shall exist," the announcement of Field's death seemed to strike a uniformly sorrowful blow. It was, indeed, not only city folk who were to feel the deep anguish caused by Field's death. A man from Aurora, Illinois, wrote to the editor of the Chicago *Times-Herald* asking if even Field had ever been aware of how much he was read and loved at country fireplaces. "It is doubtful," noted the writer, "if he knew how many aspiring young elocutionists contributed to local parlor or church entertainments with recitations of such poems as 'Little Boy Blue' and 'Knee Deep.' There is a larger percentage of reading people in the country than in the city," added the writer, "and, being lovers of nature, they could not resist the laughing meadow-brooks of the sunny Field."

Field's "laughing meadow-brooks," however, had an equally strong attraction for those living in the city—and, perhaps, with even greater reason. On the morning of November 5, when virtually hundreds of thousands would learn of Field's death for the first time as they opened their morning papers, they would find sensational murders and kidnappings, together with robberies and sex crimes, competing with the tragedy of Eugene Field for their attention. In Omaha, a city rapidly losing its reputation as a "country" town, eleven-year-old Ida Gaskin's body had been found "outraged and mutilated" in an outbuilding at the rear of her home. The alleged murderer proved to be George Morgan, the downstairs neighbor. And in New York, where "meadow-brooks" were even scarcer than in Omaha, a front-page headline in the New York *Times* told with frightening brevity a story which was becoming only too familiar for many city dwellers: FATAL COLLISION IN BROOKLYN: RAILROAD ENGINE ANNIHILATED A BREWERY TRUCK, KILLING THE DRIVER. The danger of being struck by a train was, in fact, so great in Chicago that a visitor the preceding year had been moved to remark that "those legless, armless men and women whom you meet on the streets are merely the mangled remnant of the massacre that is constantly going on year in and year out."

For Chicagoans, the morning of November 5 would bring word that the same railway company which boasted the fastest time yet to San Francisco (leaving Chicago at 6 p.m. daily and arriving in San Francisco, non-stop, on the third day at 7:45 p.m.) was also being accused of laying track on Sundays in the heart of Chicago in order to avoid safety regulations. The competing attractions of their machines and their meadows, which so engaged late-nineteenth-century intellectuals on a theoretical level, presented a daily and harrowing reality to readers of the daily press.

On one hand, "Packingtown" was considered by 1895 to be one of the great industrial achievements of the modern world. Visitors to the more than 340 acres devoted to systematic processing of meat were invited to take part in "the din of activity from city and yards which are the business man's anthem." Yet, few who did partake of this activity could ignore the disconcerting moans of the animals on their way to slaughter. In all this hum of activity, where were the forsaken "meadow-brooks"?

Joseph Medill, speaking before a noon memorial service at the Chicago Press Club on November 5, expressed the sorrow felt by many. Field "impelled us to retrace the stream of time to the period of day dreams and exuberant fancies," recalled Medill, "before cankering cares and disappointments began to embitter life.

His beautiful verses recall the images and the sentiments we then saw, and felt, and believed to be true."

Few readers, upon finishing the account of Ida Gaskin or scanning the daily tally at the stockyards, would turn to Stephen Crane's *Maggie* or Hamlin Garland's *Main-Travelled Roads.* They were more apt to turn for solace to the poems of Eugene Field. On the morning of November 5, in place of Field's usual social satire column of "Sharps and Flats" on the editorial page of the Chicago *Record,* readers were treated to the reproductions of his two most familiar poems—"Little Boy Blue" and "Wynken, Blynken and Nod." The drowsy messages of these two poems, with their suggestion of a better life elsewhere, had a natural appeal to parents who all too often had lost their children. These deaths, while perhaps less violent, were no less heartrending than Ida Gaskin's. Such common ailments as dysentery and diphtheria were reportedly on the rise in November 1895. Assistant Health Commissioner Reilly, the day before paying his condolences to Mrs. Field, had filed his monthly statement with the city of Chicago. The report indicated that during October there had been 258 deaths from diphtheria in the city, against 169 for the same month in 1894, marking a shocking increase of 53 per cent.

Mothers and fathers were continually forced to face such grim statistics as they stood helplessly watching their own children's cruel dying. The fascination, then, of Field's "Little Boy Blue," who was apparently lent by God and roused from sleep by an "angel song," was not only strong, but uncommonly compelling. The sentiment of the white-haired old man, recalled by Jean Blewett in the December issue of *Current Literature,* was perfectly understandable to most readers in the winter of 1895. After the "stilled laughter," and the "folding of baby hands," the man was found to be reading not his Bible (though it lay close by), but a newspaper. "You see," the man replied to Jean Blewett, "I've been reading of another old grandfather who had to go on living for a spell after he had lost his sunshine, and the man who wrote it—he seems —to kind of know—just—how—it feels." Though Field was, in fact, not a grandfather, he was perfectly capable of providing a grandfatherly solace for the heartbroken in their time of anguish.

For Field's followers, his death at the peak of his career seemed to mark just one more uncertainty at a time when many were rapidly growing to accept the prospect of an indifferent universe. At Niagara Falls, where transcendental souls had long accustomed themselves to reviving their faith in nature's Sublime, James Hodges was reported to have committed suicide when he jumped from near the center of Bath Island Bridge into the rapids. "The onlookers were powerless to stop him, and watched him as he was carried along by the rushing water over the last reef between the bridge and the falls, and then suddenly the body lodged there just below Every Rock and just above Chapin Island." Such lurid descriptions, detailed to the smallest incidental, seemed to many to refute any possible belief in the innate goodness of an orderly universe. Even the best-intentioned individuals could hardly alter the destinies of their fellow men.

By 1895, the anarchism of the Haymarket rioters and the feudalism of George Pullman had impressed upon Chicagoans the failure of traditional capitalistic standards when applied to the realities of city living. The year before, William T. Stead in his controversial exposé, *If Christ Came to Chicago,* had reported that America now had 4,074 millionaires who owned 20 per cent of the nation's wealth—or, in other words, the same as 11,593,887 "average" families.

There had been a time when Chicagoans had felt somehow immune to the extravagant displays of East Coast plutocrats. When George Pullman opened the Pullman Library in 1883, Dr. David Swing of Chicago's Central Church had noted that "there is nothing inexplicable or mysterious in the gold applied by the founder of this library. But should this gentleman give a Vanderbilt Ball [as had recently been done in New York at a cost of many thousands of dollars] we might well be amazed. We hope the rich men of the West will always prefer libraries, and parks, and music temples, and even good theatres to the perishable display of the ballroom."

Such hopes seemed to be borne out, at least for a time. Even in 1892, six years after the Haymarket Riots, when Mrs. Vanderbilt was spending eleven million dollars on building and furnishing "Marble House" at Newport, Chicagoans were made aware that with considerably less, George Pullman had created his own community for more than 8,000 residents, complete with shops, public halls, churches, and parks. The town, billed as a "national shrine," attracted thousands of distinguished men and women who flocked to Chicago in 1893 to see the World's Fair and also to visit the town that Pullman built. But then, in late 1893, came the full force of the Depression. And by 1894, Chicagoans were shocked as their western sky darkened with the smoke of burning railroad cars during the Pullman Strike. And a short while later, they found their spectacular World's Fair grounds invaded by members of Coxey's dishevelled army; their city once again mercilessly denied its transitory luster.

Despite such disheartening circumstances, or perhaps because of them, many Americans seemed more than willing, by November of 1895, to indulge their fantasies in periodic displays of pageantry. On the morning of November 5, few newspaper readers could avoid noting two religious ceremonies scheduled for the following day. One was to be an occasion of celebration: the marriage, at St. Thomas's Episcopal Church in New York, of Miss Consuelo Vanderbilt and the Duke of Marlborough. The other, at Chicago's Fourth Presbyterian Church, would be a somber affair—the funeral of Eugene Field. Both events represented, in a peculiar way, the end of American youthfulness. And in both cases, Americans looked to the ensuing events with almost irresistible curiosity.

The Vanderbilt-Marlborough marriage was hailed as the third wedding of a noble Churchill to an American bride and the 138th wedding of an American woman to a titled foreigner. Julian Ralph, a correspondent for the New York *Morning Journal* and a close friend of Field's, missed the funeral for the sake of the wedding. For Ralph the wedding represented a beautiful exhibition: the combination of superb taste combined with warranted indulgence. It was, in his words, nothing less than "a national triumph."

Such unabashed accolades did not, however, go entirely unchallenged. A few days earlier, on November 1, Eugene Field had noted with characteristic western pride that "the vulgarity which has characterized every phase in the Vanderbilt-Marlborough affair has never been equalled by any performance of which the woolly west has been capable up to the present time." And an article in the current issue of *Scribner's,* perhaps foreseeing the ado which would be made over the Vanderbilt wedding, severely criticized American newspapers for chronicling the lives of "decadent" New York aristocrats with descriptions of "the number of bottles of champagne opened at the marriage of some millionaire's daughter." This same article, in seeking an answer to the question of "What is an American?," found the qualities truest to the national grain to be naturalness, self-respect, success, and character—precisely those traits which Eugene Field had come to embody in the popular imagination.

With the burial of Field and the marriage of Consuelo Vanderbilt, many Americans could not help but feel the inevitable pain of aging. How could one retain faith in the sanctity of marriage or the honest values of family living when the daughters of America's revered plutocrats were so easily lured away by the fortune-hunting sons of Europe's nobility—when, almost simultaneously, the nation's "Children's Laureate," himself the father of five children, could be stricken dead at the premature age of forty-five. Both Consuelo Vanderbilt and Eugene Field seemed, in many respects, to be victims of a commercial society. The same trains which represented the misspent wealth of the Vanderbilts were now rushing through the streets of the city, forcing Chicagoans like Field to flee to newly-formed suburbs and serving as daily reminders that technology could as easily become a curse as a blessing.

At 2 o'clock on November 6, just as the Duke and Duchess of Marlborough were leaving St. Thomas's Church in New York, funeral services were being held for Eugene Field in the Fourth Presbyterian Church at Rush and Superior streets in downtown Chicago. Once inside the church, visitors found themselves surrounded by an overwhelming display of flowers. Roses, chrysanthemums, and lilies so completely surrounded the bier, in fact, that many of Field's friends found no place for their personal contributions. Lavish arrangements were described by the press, including: a shoe of white carnations with the inscribed words

"Wynken, Blynken and Nod"; a "handsome" trumpet and drum of violets and roses sent by the president and board of managers of the Union League Club; a seven-foot-high harp of chrysanthemums and roses sent by the State's Attorney Jacob J. Kern; and—a "most touching remembrance"—a pen and scroll of white carnations sent by the Fellowship Club bearing in heliotrope the words: "This is not death, only a change of scene."

In the eyes of one Field crony, it was a "gaudy, effusive, Chicago funeral—such a one as in his working days in the newspaper editorial rooms Eugene would have lampooned with as much sarcastic vim as he was wont to display wherever snobbery reared its head." But beyond the pageantry, Field's devoted followers admired the exquisite touches of simplicity which accompanied the burial.

One widely circulated story told of the single white rose—the gift of love, without money and without price—which occupied the place of honor, resting in Field's hand. The preceding day, so the story went, a woman had entered a florist's shop to buy a wreath for the poet. A moment later, a poorly clad little girl entered and asked: "Are those flowers for Mr. Field? Oh, I wish I could send him just one. Won't you please give me one flower?"

The florist placed the finest white rose in her hand. Then she turned and gave it to the lady, requesting: "Please put it near Mr. Field with your flowers." And so it came to be told and retold that this single white rose was buried with Field, held in the fingers that had done so much for childhood.

The formal services—conducted by the Reverend Thomas C. Hall with the Reverend Frank W. Gunsaulus reading the prayer and the Reverend F. M. Bristol giving the eulogy—opened with a choral rendition of Field's popular poem "Singing in God's Acre." The choir began:

Out yonder in the moonlight, wherein God's Acre lies,
Go angels walking to and fro, singing their lullabies.
Their radiant wings are folded, and their eyes bended low,
As they sing among the beds wherein the flowers delight to grow.

Dr. Bristol then commented on the familiar Eugene Field of the laughing "meadow-brooks" and the parallels which could be drawn with the Holy Savior. "He had the spirit which was also in Him who loved the flowers of the field and the birds of the air, and who took the little children up in His arms and put His hands upon them and blessed them." Dr. Bristol continued that this same spirit, manifested in the poet, could be imagined "as seating a little child in our midst to teach us in the midst of our bustling of city building and fortune building, the greatness of faith, hope and love; the greatness of the child spirit."

For Dr. Bristol the values represented by Field were the human qualities now threatened by the push of the city. Field was seen as the eternal boy-Christ, the natural man, who lived in the city, and ministered to humanity with his poetry, and yet remained uncorrupted by it all. Even in death, Field had managed to retain that joyous exuberance of boyhood. In Dr. Bristol's words, Field had never lost "the reverence for sacred things learned in childhood. The streams of his happy songs, the happiness of heaven, which were instilled into his heart when but a boy."

For those gathered in Chicago's Fourth Presbyterian Church on November 6, 1895, it seemed apparent that death for Field could not mean *real* death, but "only a change of scene." The ever-present theme of Field's poetry had, after all, been that death for the innocent, the child, was not punishment but rather the gate to everlasting life. And the viewer, then, should not mourn, but rather should use the occasion to ponder the weakness of man in God's eyes, as well as the state of his own transgressions. Field had miraculously escaped the grip of Chicago's undertow, but could others say as much? What hope was there for *their* souls?

Dr. Bristol concluded his remarks by imploring that "some day, out in God's acre, where angels sing their 'Sleep, Oh, Sleep,' a monument shall mark the resting-place of our gentle poet; and let it be built, as was Daniel Defoe's in London, by the loving, grateful contributions of the children of the land." It took but this one sentence from Dr. Bristol's funeral oration to arouse the sympathies of Field's young friends on the subject of a monument to their lost laureate.

Then, in leaving the church, "his humbler friends did all they could to show their love, and with tear-bathed eyes they looked into his dead face, and with trembling lips whispered, 'Good-bye.'"

The Eugene Field House

Field's den was described by reporters as "the most wonderful room in all the city." Buena Park, Illinois, *c.* 1895.

The Eugene Field House

The poet's "Sabine Farm" library contained a complete collection of works on Horace. Buena Park, Illinois, *c.* 1895.

Chicago Historical Society

The John Hiltman family was one of the first to hear of Field's death. Buena Park, Illinois, *c.* 1895.

Chicago Historical Society

The journalist's sentimental verse provided a welcome relief for those caught in the rush of city living. State Street, Chicago, 1893.

Longhorn cattle awaiting slaughter. Union Stock Yards, Chicago, 1892.

Chicago Historical Society

Chicago Historical Society

The child of the late nineteenth century was looked upon as a symbol of "faith, hope, and love." Burned railroad cars, Pullman, Illinois, 1894.

New York Public Library

Consuelo Vanderbilt with the coronet of her husband's
house of Marlborough. Her marriage took place on the
day Field was buried.

Eugene Field and Julian Ralph at Pewaukee Lake, Wisconsin. Ralph, a correspondent for the New York *Morning Journal,* missed Field's funeral for the sake of the wedding.

Denver Public Library

Denver Public Library

Field visiting the "laughing meadow-brooks" of George Yenowine's Wisconsin farm, *c.* 1894.

Monuments, Memorials, and House Restorations

By Christmas 1925—thirty years after Field's death and the same year in which Field's Buena Park home yielded reluctantly to the city's indomitable wrecking ball—Chicagoans took heart in the fact that the monument suggested by Dr. Bristol in his funeral address now stood proudly, and presumably securely, in Chicago's Lincoln Park. If the monument had not been built entirely as was Defoe's—"by the loving, grateful contributions of the children"— that seemed of little importance in light of the singular beauty of the sculptured masterpiece and the strong impressions such a memorial would have on generations yet to come.

The monument itself—consisting of the bronze statue of "The Rock-a-By Lady from Hush-a-By Street," a fountain, and two marble seats—stood not far from the animal house in the park. As such, it marked not only the culmination of the efforts of Field's younger friends but also the philanthropic gestures of Field's older companions who, with the passing of the years, increased their donations faithfully.

In the initial stages, contributions to the monument fund had been recorded by the nine Chicago newspapers which accepted the responsibility for sponsoring Dr. Bristol's suggestion. By the time of the funeral, in fact, the Chicago *Record* had reported a total of $62.70 already accounted for—the pride of fifty-eight young donors. In each case, the child's name or that of his parents, the amount given, and often a few lines—many of them containing childish queries on the life hereafter—were listed. Nine-year-old Lillian Dawson sent twenty-five cents for the children's fund and asked unabashedly if, since Field was now dead, would Santa Claus have any of Field's books this Christmas? And six-year-old C. Carroll Cobb wrote: "Ernest is our baby brother and we call him Little Boy Blue. I hope the angels won't take our Little Boy Blue the way they took Mr. Field's. Our little Bessie will see Mr. Field in heaven, don't you think so?"

More often than not, the child subscriber was too young to write his own tribute, and a mother or father would attempt to explain the youngster's sentiments. Five-year-old Arthur J. Hiester's parents, for example, enclosed fifty cents, noting that "when the Field monument project was mentioned to him he at once became very enthusiastic and decided to contribute his little savings to that. He always loved to hear his mamma and papa read the dead poet's childhood verses to him, one of his favorites being the 'Dinky Bird,' which his mother often sings to him. Please credit this amount to Arthur J. Hiester."

There can be little doubt that the children's enthusiasm for Field was given strong, if not overwhelming, support by loyal parents. As Field's friend and biographer, Francis Wilson, noted in reviewing Field's *A Little Book of Profitable Tales,* "Children, as a rule, become discouraged when in the course of a single volume of tales, however beautifully written, so many of their little heroes and heroines die." And even Field himself had once remarked, "I have no particular desire to shine as a writer for small children." Perhaps, then, if there was a particular reason for Field's popularity, it arose not so much from the children's assistance as their parents' remembrance. A writer for the Kansas City *Star* noted Field "wrote so that a grown-up—be he ever so old and ever so far removed from the mystery of the child world—could see and understand and find in his heart once more the fleeting days of his childhood." And with the advent of the twentieth century, many found these days to be an even rarer enjoyment than before. The model of innocent child life stood as a kind of lost refuge which many felt could no longer be regained, but which should, in any case, be preserved whenever possible.

One such preservationist was Slason Thompson who, in 1913, joined his friend Will J. Davis, Sr., on a visit to Field's grave. A reporter from the *Inter Ocean Magazine* was there to record the incident. "September 2 was the poet's birthday," he noted, and, while the "event was forgotten for the most part in the driving grind of the loop district, Will J. Davis, Sr. and Slason Thompson remembered. They went out to Graceland cemetery to offer their homage to his last resting place." What the two men found proved dismaying. At the consecrated ground they discovered a small, plain headstone of gray granite; the poet's name, with his birth and death dates, afforded the only inscription. As Davis explained in an interview, "It isn't that the grave is neglected but we feel that it is a public duty to do something more. Our plan at present is to erect over the grave a simple but noble shaft, carved with some excerpts from Field's poetry. Besides this," he added, "we want to erect a statue in one of the parks, preferably Lincoln Park, where he used to go almost every morning in the summer to play with the children."

Adults, upon this cue, quickly picked up the neglected baton of the children's crusade. A new monument committee was created, reuniting such old Field cronies as the bookdealer Frank Morris and Dr. Frank Gunsaulus, along with Slason Thompson and Will J. Davis, Sr. By the War's end, another $4,379.80 had been added to the coffer which, when combined with the $5,540.45 previously raised, qualified the memorial group for sufficient funds from Chicago's Ferguson Foundation to consummate the project.

A few years after the monument's belated completion, Field's Chicago followers met once again. This time, in 1926, the setting was the affluent Church of the Holy Comforter in suburban Kenilworth where it was seen fit to place Field's body in a location more dignified than Graceland Cemetery could possibly provide. As the men and women stood about in the bitter cold, Judge Jesse Holdom of the Superior Court delivered the eulogy address. "Eugene Field," noted the judge, "passed out of this world as he had lived in it—a lover of little children. He went to the world beyond as a little child, loving them and striving for them and inspiring them by his imperishable poems to strive for the ideals of life."

As the service closed, Judge Holdom recited the immortal "Little Boy Blue." The body was then lowered into the elaborate churchyard tomb by the honorary pallbearers, including Chicago's Mayor William Dever, Northwestern University President Walter Dill Scott, and the author Henry Blake Fuller. A marble slab, inscribed simply "Eugene Field, 1850–1895, the Children's Poet," was placed atop the sacred ground.

Despite such substantial acts of good faith as the Lincoln Park statue and the Kenilworth tomb, there were, nonetheless, those who were dismayed by the promotional aspects of these gestures. "Field means nothing at all to the generation born since 1895," lamented one reporter. "To them he is scarcely a name, and what interest the youth of Chicago manifests is one that has been artificially prompted by teachers and newspapers."

It was obvious to most, however, that Chicago did not stand alone in its susceptibility to classroom and newspaper promotion. At almost the same time that plans were completed for the monument in Lincoln Park, similar proposals were begun in half a dozen cities across the United States. Denver, in fact, claimed honors for erecting the first park memorial when Mrs. Mabel Landrum Torrey, in 1919, designed a seven-foot-high marble statue of Wynken, Blynken and Nod for the city's Washington Park. Soon after, in both Denver and St. Louis, battles were revived to save the homes where Field had once lived. In St. Joseph, the city fathers decided to devote their energies to the gathering and care of the Field manuscripts which should "rightfully be in St. Joseph." School and library dedications, statues, and biographies and autobiographies mentioning Field all flourished throughout the Twenties.

Much of the Field revival at this time arose from the same conditions which had created such a strong sense of loss at the time of his death. While the Nineties had been plagued by anarchism, decadent robber barons, and irresponsible railroads, the Twenties saw the growth of the Klan, speakeasies, and an enormous increase in the use of the automobile. Both decades would be viewed by many as low-points in the nation's ethical well-being. If, in the Nineties, unchecked wealth had made it possible for Consuelo Vanderbilt to depart with the Duke of Marlborough, the proliferation of the automobile, in the Twenties, made it possible for virtually anyone's daughter to be whisked off in virtually anyone else's rumble seat. Morality could no longer be chaperoned. Instead, preservers of Field's reputation felt that morality must be learned through example. And there was no longer time to wait for the children's crusade.

It seems no accident that whenever circumstances permitted, the house—as an embodiment of family stability—was picked as the fitting tribute to Eugene Field. In the twentieth century, more than the physical structure was at stake when a house fell prey to demolition squads. More often than not these dwellings were replaced by either smaller houses or apartment buildings. The fate of Ida Gaskin at her neighbor's hand—so obviously a victim of crowded conditions in the Nineties—could only be multiplied in the Twenties. What chance was there for backyard communion when a giant apartment house crowded the landscape—as was the case in Field's own backyard by the early Twenties. By 1925, when Field's Buena Park house was destroyed, it was impossible to imagine the neighborly good will demonstrated at the time of his death.

But more serious than the decline of neighborliness was the coinciding threat to traditional home values created when women were cut free from the drudgeries of maintaining a large household. When smaller houses and apartments were built, they became easier to look after and, simultaneously, easier to escape.

An article which had appeared in the *Ladies' Home Journal* at the time of Field's death on how to entertain and make an ideal home for "the dearest boy" (meaning the husband) with only one maid, would, by the Twenties, seem laughably irrelevant. In the suburbs adjacent to Buena Park, Frank Lloyd Wright had designed the "prairie-style" house whose kitchen and service areas served as the prototype for making lighter work of the preparation of meals. By the Twenties, vacuum cleaners, electric washing-machines, and electric irons helped free the average housewife from previously endless domestic chores. Part-time jobs outside the house became commonplace. And women, with a feeling of comparative social and economic independence, inevitably championed suffrage. While perhaps just as inevitable were the efforts on the part of certain individuals to restore the home as shrine.

In St. Louis, such a shrine was found at 634 South Broadway. It made little difference to those seeking restoration of the house throughout the Twenties that contrary to the outside wall plaque the house was not, in fact, Field's birthplace. Mark Twain had made the significance of the house explicitly clear when he officiated at the ceremony for the placement of the plaque in 1902. Just before the dedicatory ceremony ended, Roswell Field, the poet's younger brother, arrived in a public carriage to announce that if the truth were known, Field's birthplace had been a house on Collins Street now occupied by a feed store. But Twain, unruffled by the intrusion, turned dolefully to the brother and said simply, "Rose, whatever the fact may be is relatively unimportant. It is the official and formal thing that counts. Officially and for the purposes of the future, your brother was born here."

And so, though the official state records were changed, the plaque which Mark Twain had dedicated remained unaltered. And years later, in 1925, when word came from St. Louis that Field's boyhood home was about to be razed for the sake of a giant warehouse, the little toy dog did not desert his post and the little toy soldier stubbornly refused his marching orders. M. P. Smith, superintendent of the Flat River, Missouri schools apparently sounded the battle cry when he wrote a letter to the editor of the St. Louis *Star*. "If it could be spared," implored the superintendent, "it eventually would become a shrine to which many people would make pilgrimages. Is there no way to stir up interest in the matter and save the house?"

Apparently there was. A few days later a letter appeared in the St. Louis *Times* signed by a grown-up "Little Boy Blue." "When I was a lad living in the East," wrote the correspondent, "I heard my teacher tell one day of the great poet, Eugene Field. I heard of Eugene Field long before I ever heard of Jesse James, gangsters, mules, breweries, corn-cob pipes, houndogs, etc., and must say I was only one of the children who thrilled at a poem of Eugene Field's in childhood moments. You can imagine," he added, "how sickened I became when my childhood hopes and dreams turned into a nightmare." There, in St. Louis, according to the correspondent, stood a "shadow of regret of a once fine residence on Broadway—showing our own forgetfulness of a rose that bloomed at home and whose perfume thrilled thousands." To regain the elusive fragrance, the writer suggested that a fund drive be started immediately for restoration of the home.

And finally an article appeared in the New York *Times* for February 17, 1935, headlined: CHILDREN'S GIFTS SAVE EUGENE FIELD SHRINE: 100,000 PUPILS IN ST. LOUIS DONATE PENNIES TO RESTORE THE POET'S BOYHOOD HOME. But once again, the story beneath the headline pointed out that the bulk of the contributions had come not from the children but, in this case, from two St. Louis insurance agents—Jesse P. Henry and Carl P. Daniel.

That these essential funds came from the business community would not seem unusual in the Thirties, when John D. Rockefeller, Henry Ford, and other businessmen were already pouring millions into historical preservation projects. And Field in particular among poets always evoked a strong following from the ranks of industry. As Lyman Gage, the Chicago banker, had put it in analyzing his own emotions almost four decades earlier at the time of Field's death:

> By the law of reaction, businessmen who spend so many hours daily amid brick and mortar surroundings, wrestling with figures and financial details, should love nature. I know I do, and for a like reason perhaps I learned to regard with tender friendship that brilliant man.

When, in Denver, means were sought to save the house where Field had lived while working as managing editor of the Denver *Tribune,* the chief benefactor and promoter to pursue the house preservation cause was the undeniably "Unsinkable" Molly Brown. In 1927, when Molly Brown announced her intention of preserving the little house on Colfax where Field had lived between 1881 and 1883, she did this because "Gene had never failed me."

> The first money I ever made was when the miners rolled silver dollars on the stage when I recited Field's poems at Leadville. When I, with Judge Lindsey, sponsored the first juvenile court at benefits, I always recited his poems. I recited his poems in New York when 2,000 assembled in the Waldorf Astoria to greet me when I came up from the Titanic disaster. I have read his poems to soldiers and miners and he has always gone over big.

If "Gene" never failed Molly, however, the time would come when the people of Denver, in spite of her efforts, would fail her. In September 1930, a United Press dispatch from Paris reported that "the ghost of Little Boy Blue is stalking the streets of Denver. And the little toy dog is shaking the dust from his back in vehement protests. It may even be imagined that the toy soldier, red from suppressed indignation rather than rust, is searching for a new musket."

What had purportedly so outraged the little toy dog and his companion soldier were the plans by the city of Denver to make way for a new apartment house on Colfax Avenue. The Field house would be moved to a nearby park where it would be used as a branch library. In Paris, Molly Brown, who had recently given the house to Denver, lamented:

> You see, we are such utilitarians at home that in spite of all our space, all our wealth, we must utilize one of our greatest poet's homes as a library. They would paint it up—put frescoes of nursery scenes on the walls, poems on the ceiling. Oh! "mais ça dépasse tout!" It was not a Lapin Agile I gave to the city of Denver.

Molly's pique at American utilitarianism provided an apt description of not only the Denver preservationists, but the Field preservation movement as a whole. By the Twenties, what had begun in 1895 as a more or less legitimate attempt to preserve the memory of the "children's laureate" had developed into unabashed moralizing. No longer content merely to preserve his memory, Field's preservationists now sought to promote the message. What the real Field had been like was unimportant. As Mark Twain had so forthrightly put it, "it was the official and formal thing that counted." Throughout the Twenties and into the Thirties, as America seemed to drift deeper and deeper into moral laxity, Field came increasingly to embody those values which stood for the wholesome side of American life.

Field had always been a popular classroom item. By the Twenties, however, what had previously been confined to classroom exercises became public manifestos, memorials, or literary tributes. Field's reputation was readjusted to meet the demands of a much-tattered American Dream.

Major Field biographies were published in 1924 and 1927. The first was Charles H. Dennis's account of *Eugene Field's Creative Years,* dealing ostensibly with Field's Chicago work but, in fact, probing much of the earlier period. The second, Slason Thompson's *Life of Eugene Field,* attempted to deal with the "whole" man. Because both authors had worked closely with Eugene Field on the Chicago *Daily News,* total objectivity was presumably never sought. Similarly, Melville E. Stone, who was Field's managing editor on the Chicago *Morning News,* and Francis Wilson, the comedian, both wrote their autobiographies in the Twenties; both included sections on Eugene Field.

The impact of these writings—combined with the memorials —brought before the American public a renewed image of the poet and journalist which spoke loudly and persistently to Americans' deepest hopes and most cherished ambitions. Melville Stone made note of the Puritan strain of Field's ancestry which provided him with a profound, even spiritual, nature. At the same time, Francis Wilson in his autobiography saw Field above all as a man worthy of letters, intensely, whimsically American. And Slason Thompson, in revising his original biography of Field, commented in 1927 on the significance of Field's "Americanness" for the twentieth century:

The secret of Eugene Field's hold upon American readers that knew him not in the flesh, and so are not interested in the quips and comments of the day, may be summed up in the single phrase —he was American. English was his tongue, but his heart was wholly American. His point of view was American. His wit, like that of Artemus Ward, was American; his irreverence for popular idols of the mart, the field and the forum was American; but above and beyond all his faith in womankind and motherhood was universal.

Field's biographers effectively recalled his boyishness and spontaneity, his penchant for good-natured practical jokes, his concern for animals, and most importantly his devotion to his wife and family. As one writer remarked in 1924 in reviewing Charles Dennis's *Creative Years:*

> This book strips the clownish garb from Field and exposes him as he really was—a lovable, kind man, who wrote poems overflowing with sentiment and love for humanity not because editors asked him for them, but because he found his greatest joy in the happiness that he gave to children.

Field was made to appear to his public as a good-hearted Adam, a friend to man and child, and more than that, the possessor himself of eternal boyishness. As Dennis recalled, "it always seemed to me that Field's attitude toward children was very like the attitude of one child toward another. He had the child's gift of wondering, and the child's delight in all things strange or beautiful." In the accelerated world of the twentieth century, Field was remembered as the self-reliant Emersonian, a man who dared to walk the children's path.

Chicago Historical Society

The completion of the Lincoln Park monument marked the culmination of the efforts of Field's younger friends along with the philanthropic gestures of his older associates. Pictured here, Jean Field Foster and Robert Eugene Field at the unveiling, October 10, 1922.

Chicago Historical Society

In 1926 Field's body was removed from Graceland Cemetery and placed in a "more dignified" setting at the Church of the Holy Comforter in suburban Kenilworth.

Winkin, Blinkin, & Nod
by Torrey

Denver Public Library

Denver claimed honors in 1919 for erecting the first park memorial dedicated to Field with its seven-foot-high statue of Wynken, Blynken and Nod.

Chicago Historical Society

There was little chance for backyard communion after Chicago's giant apartment houses began crowding the landscape in the twentieth century. Field and friend, Buena Park, *c.* 1894.

Missouri Historical Society

Mark Twain remained unruffled in 1902 after Field's brother Roswell interrupted the dedication ceremonies by saying that the St. Louis house was not, in fact, Field's birthplace.

The Eugene Field House

The house claimed as Field's birthplace in St. Louis prior to restoration efforts of the twentieth century.

Insurance Agent Jesse P. Henry met with St. Louis School Superintendent Henry J. Gerling to inspect the restoration of the house known as Field's birthplace.

The Eugene Field House

Denver Public Library

The house where Field had lived in Denver was saved by Molly Brown only to be moved to a city park in 1930 to make way for a new apartment house on Colfax Avenue.

Denver Public Library

The "Unsinkable" Molly Brown in Paris, 1930, where she
lamented that "we are such utilitarians at home that . . .
we must utilize one of our greatest poet's homes as a
library."

Youth:
ħomes and ħouses

The year following Field's death marked the publication of the complete, ten-volume *Writings in Prose and Verse of Eugene Field*. A fitting tribute, it seemed, for the man hailed as America's "Children's Laureate." Commenting on the collected works for the *Atlantic Monthly,* the reviewer proclaimed, "He has written the Canterbury Pilgrimage of infancy." Adding that, unfortunately, because of Field's untimely death, "the great book of human interpretation is the poorer . . . the tale had to be left half told."

Joel Chandler Harris echoed similar sentiments in his introduction for volume eight, entitled *The House.*

> We are told, alas! that the story of Alice and Reuben Baker wanted but one chapter to complete it when Eugene Field died. That chapter was to have told how they reached the fulfillment of their heart's desire. But even here the unities are preserved. The

chapter that is unwritten in the book is also unwritten in the lives of perhaps the great majority of men and women.

For most readers it appeared obvious that Reuben Baker was none other than a thinly disguised pseudonym for Eugene Field and that Reuben Baker's house, like Field's own, was both mythical and, at the same time, real.

As was the case with virtually all Field's writings, *The House* was first published in serial form in the "Sharps and Flats" column of the *Daily News*. For the several months preceding his death, Field's readers had been treated to a humorous but exasperating description of the obstacles confronting a Chicago couple in their attempted move to the suburbs. As the Bakers' dreams rapidly "simmered and shrivelled down from the Norman-Gothic to plain, everyday, fin-de-siècle architecture," Field's readers found themselves hopelessly—albeit enjoyably—embroiled in the Bakers' mirth-filled episodes with unreliable workmen, persistent salesmen, and their well-meaning, but over-anxious, neighbors-to-be. Ultimately, with Field's unexpected death, the Bakers (along with Field's readers) were left disappointingly stranded on what seemed the unstepped thresholds of their individual dreams.

In real life, the fictional dilemma of the Reuben Bakers—left bereft of hearth and home—could only serve as a rude parody of Field's own life. As Slason Thompson pointed out about Field's celebrated Buena Park home, "the photographs taken a few months before his death of Eugene Field's home and the beautiful library in which he wrote are ghastly travesties on the nomadic character of his domestic arrangements."

Field's entire life, until he moved into his so-called "Sabine

Farm," had, in fact, been spent in either cramped apartments or small, rented houses. The first house he actually owned was that in Buena Park—where he moved five months prior to his death. And although the "home," as such, had come to represent the virtual embodiment of Field's reputation in the popular imagination, in point of actual fact, Field's upbringing had been notably devoid of strong familial ties. The houses—so fervently restored by the teachers, newspaper reporters, and historical preservationists in the Twenties and early Thirties—could, for the most part, serve only to emphasize the poverty of Field's own home experience. His early family relationships had generally been tenuous and brief and it was only in his later years—with the emergence of his own family —that any semblance of family unity developed.

The St. Louis house—saved in the early Thirties by two St. Louis insurance agents—must have represented for Field only memories of great sorrow. It was, after all, while living in this house that Field witnessed first the deaths of his own brothers and sisters, and finally the death of his mother in 1856. After Field was born—and *not* before as popular belief would have it—his parents moved from a house on Collins Street to the later renovated house at 634 South Broadway. In the eight years of their wedded life in St. Louis, Field's parents gave birth to eight children, but —as was all too common in mid-century America—only two of them survived infancy. And then, when Field was six, his mother died of cholera.

The boys' father, Roswell Martin Field, was a scholarly lawyer with apparently little time for the boys. After his mother's death, young Eugene and his brother, Roswell, were sent East to live with relatives. And although his father at this time received a certain degree of fame for his early defense of Dred Scott, this fame meant little for the young Field. After 1856, Eugene would never again live in the same house with his father and such correspondence as existed between the two was often carried on in formal Latin until his father's own premature death in 1869.

It is not surprising that in all Field's childhood verse, there is little commenting upon his *own* early childhood in St. Louis. It was not until he reached the age of forty that Field wrote his first, and only, poetic tribute to his mother. The poem, entitled simply "To My Mother," appeared initially in the October 25, 1890 column of "Sharps and Flats." The poem begins:

> How fair you are, my mother!
>   Ah, though 'tis many a year
>   Since you were here,
> Still do I see your beauteous face,
>   And with the glow
> Of your dark eyes cometh a grace
>   Of long ago.

Field apparently never forgot his mother who was described by his sister-in-law Ida Comstock Below as being "a very handsome woman, possessed of great strength."

According to popular legend, Roswell Senior's prime consideration in sending his boys to Amherst was that they should be brought up in the "nurture and admonition of the Lord"—and free of the superstitions of New England. The person given responsibility for fulfilling this task was Eugene's maiden cousin, Mary Field French, of Amherst, occasionally assisted by his paternal grandmother in Newfane, Vermont. Field's dedication to his *Little Book of Western Verse,* provides the most intimate, if sentimental, insight into Field's move to Amherst.

To Mary Field French

A dying mother gave to you
    Her child a many years ago;
How in your gracious love he grew,
    You know, dear, patient heart, you know.

The mother's child you fostered then
    Salutes you now and bids you take
These little children of his pen
    And love them for the author's sake.

Of course it was not Field's dying mother but his very much alive and preoccupied father who in actual fact had given the young Field to Miss French. Nonetheless, the poem testifies to Field's enduring attachment to Mary French. In the words of Dr. James Tufts, Eugene's tutor, Miss French was "always sociable and agreeable and so admirably adapted. to the charge of the two brothers. Here in this charming home, under the best of New England influences and religious instruction, with nothing harsh or repulsive, the boys could not have found a more congenial home."

The loving care of Miss French notwithstanding, there was something in Field which rebelled against his puritanical surroundings. A letter to his cousin Julia in 1879 stands in stark contrast to his much later comment to Hamlin Garland that his Amherst days were "the sweetest and finest days of my life." In this letter, Field complained bitterly to his cousin about the hardships involved in maintaining the "best" of New England influences:

There doesn't seem to be any prospect of getting Mary French away from the old home. I fail to recognize any bliss in vegetating in that humdrum, old foggy hamlet of Amherst. When God Almighty visited the place with fire, it's a pity he didn't complete the job. But as he is in the habit of doing a good many things my human intellect can't grasp, I will not subject him to unfriendly criticism.

Such incongruous "ways of the Lord" were made most apparent during Field's visits to his grandmother's house in Newfane, Vermont. And particularly incongruous to the young Field was the difference in privilege which existed between the elect and the not-so-elect in the local Congregational church. "My lovely old grandmother," wrote Field some years later, "was one of the very elect. How many times have I carried her footstove for her and filled it in the vestry room. I have frozen in the old pew while grandma kept nice and warm and nibbled lozenges and cassia cakes during the meeting." In an article Field wrote for the *Ladies' Home Journal,* he recalled:

> Yes, grandma was Puritanical—not to the extent of persecution, but a Puritan in the severity of her faith and in the exacting nicety of her interpretation of her duties to God and mankind. Grandma's Sunday began at six o'clock Saturday evening; by that hour her house was swept and garnished, and her lamps trimmed, every preparation made for a quiet, reverential observance of the Sabbath Day.

Ultimately, then, in accordance with his father's early wishes, Field seems to have emerged from his New England years relatively free of Yankee "superstitions" while retaining a keen remembrance of the stuffiness of his Eastern elders. Years later, while working for the Chicago *Morning News,* Field would write:

> Down East they have a great regard for what they call "atmosphere," [but] a Western man does not depend upon "atmosphere," and therefore he is not likely to believe in it. His loathing of "atmosphere" is intensified when he visits the East and breathes and smells what manner of thing this so-called "atmosphere" is— a sticky incense burned continually before narrow, vainglorious intellectual pigmies by busy little parasites.

By 1868, when Field attended Williams College for a year, he defiantly rejected the instructional attempts of his teachers. As Dr. Tufts' wife later recalled, "He was too smart for the professors at Williams; because they did not understand him, they could not pardon his eccentricities." Field, obviously, had already begun indulging his life-long penchant for practical jokes, and, as might be expected, before the end of his freshman year the stalwart faculty at Williams decided that Field had too little time for learning to be a desirable student. He was promptly sent back to the patient Dr. Tufts at Monson.

The following year, Field's father died, and Eugene went to join his guardian, Professor John Burgess, at Knox College in Galesburg, Illinois. During the Civil War, Knox College—which had been founded in 1837 by Rev. George Washington Gale of the Oneida Institute—became well known in abolitionists' circles as one of the principal Underground Railroad stations in Illinois. The list of abolitionists who visited and lectured there is impressive: Theodore Parker, Wendell Phillips, Cassius M. Clay, John P. Hale, Henry Ward Beecher, and William Lloyd Garrison. And during the Reconstruction period after the war, according to at least one writer, "The students and teachers attracted to Knox were on the whole devoted to the same religious and moral principles as had been the founders of the college."

Standing in marked contrast to the typical student, in 1869, was Eugene Field. Living off the early dividends of his patrimony —estimated variously at between $6,000 and $60,000—Field already showed the incipient tastes for extravagant decoration which were to later characterize the celebrated room in Chicago. Charles Dennis, in terms strikingly similar to those employed in November of 1895, noted that Field's fellow students at Knox were "dazzled" by his quarters at Galesburg's leading hotel where he was surrounded by strange and peculiar objects and a library of considerable size.

No doubt Field's Galesburg furnishings were, in part, a compensation for an absence of any real home in his childhood and a reaction against the strict observance of puritanical duties which pervaded his grandmother's Newfane house. Ultimately, the religious orthodoxy of Galesburg left an impression on Field not too dissimilar from that of Amherst. In a humorous, though seemingly earnest article which Field wrote years later, he noted:

Galesburg takes life seriously and with imposing solemnity. She abhors and eschews every worldly vanity, and the only excess in which she indulges is the planting and cultivation of rose bushes. Rose bushes everywhere—in the streets, over the lawns, all through the gardens. . . . If ever a scandal invades this delectable community it is kept strictly sub-rosa, and all things carnal, spiritual, temporal, and eternal are glinted and tinted with couleur de rose. These rose bushes and these roses lend their characteristics to the community itself, so that however fragrant may be the memory one has of Galesburg it is always a thorn that pins that memory to the heart.

Charles Dennis, in his biography of Field, suggests that these remarks stemmed from the time Field's hotel room caught fire and perhaps Field had in mind the loss of his beloved father's letters. A more realistic episode, however, is that to which Field referred in a letter he wrote to Julia prior to their marriage in 1872. In the letter Field confessed the story of his "other love"—a young girl named Maggie Bowers who attended Knox Seminary at the same time Field attended the college. In Field's words:

> She was pretty and vivacious and was smart. I was wild and dissipated and her parents did not favor me. [They] were secretly endeavoring to break the match . . . they circulated a rumor that I blush to think of. A rumor that implicated my honor and good name, those jewels beyond all price! Maggie wrote me a letter and I saw that her mind had been poisoned and I knew that we could never be happy. So I then and there told her we must part forever.

Although Field judiciously avoided divulging the precise nature of the rumor, there can be little doubt that this episode not only heightened Field's awareness of the hypocrisy of Victorian morality but also encouraged his transfer the next year to the University of Missouri in Columbia where his brother was enrolled as a junior.

At Missouri, away from the direct supervision of Professor Burgess and the stringent social conventions of Galesburg, Field felt freer to indulge his puckish spirit. A classmate would later recall that he was a "typical carefree American schoolboy, his brain always teeming with schemes to make fun for others as well as himself and his waking hours so devoted to pranks that it was a mystery when he ever found time for study." At Columbia, Field not only failed his math class but was almost expelled from the University in 1871 after conducting a raid on the president's wine cellar. The occasion was not, however, without its literary import since it served as inspiration for what has been labeled as "Field's first printed poem." The final lines of this poem, in mock Latin, proclaim:

> The frightened pueri all crowd,
> Around the Doctor, who aloud,
> Proclaims ut he will have to see,
> Them ranged before the Faculty.
> Sed gloria to that Faculty.
> Doctor cavet, pueri, free.

On another occasion, Field displayed his unparalleled skill at masquerading. A family friend, Mrs. J. S. Branham, recalled the time she was relaxing on the front porch of her father's old home in Columbia when a strangely dressed woman appeared wearing a hoop skirt, a beribboned bonnet, and waving a large fan. "To our surprise," remembered the friend, "she mounted the low fence in front of our house and cakewalked from one end of it to the other, singing the ridiculous song, 'Old Aunt Jemima, Oh, High, Oh.'" The peculiar woman, to no one's amazement, was later discovered to have been Eugene Field.

Although Field did not begin his professional writing career until 1873, when he went to work for the St. Louis *Journal,* he had, by this time, already shown considerable writing ability. While at Knox he had written several humorous articles about campus events for the Galesburg *Register,* and even before arriving at Knox he had sent a most revealing letter to Lillie Olmstead of Williamstown, Massachusetts. "If I act in accordance with the wishes of my friends," wrote Field, "I shall enter upon the practice of the law." But, he added, "it is not my wish to do so, although I have expressed my opinion but to a few. It is my pet scheme to become a Journalist, and I trust my hopes may be realized eventually." For the next several years, however, these wishes lay dormant.

In the meantime, during Field's stay at the University of Missouri he made his initial acquaintance with the couple who were to serve as his surrogate parents for many of his remaining years. Melvin L. Gray, a lawyer living in St. Louis, in accepting the executorship of Field's father's estate, received the responsibility for distributing Eugene's patrimony. Years later, on the occasion of Mrs. Gray's death in 1891, Field wrote about the unique influence of their home life:

> I was at that time (1871) just coming of age, and there were many reasons why I was attracted to the home over which this admirable lady presided. In the first place, Mrs. Gray's household was a counterpart of the household to which my boyhood life in New England had attached me. Mrs. Gray [was] a friend as indulgent, as forbearing, as sympathetic, as kindly suggestive and as disinterested as a mother, and in her home [was found] a refuge from temptation, care and vexation.

That Field should seek a refuge "from temptation, care and vexation" does not seem unusual in light of his earlier experiences. For most of the years preceding Field's acquaintance with the Grays, Field's homes—by means of their moral supervision—

had served only to whet his freedom-loving appetite. In the Grays' household, Field found an environment that was—by the very nature of its semi-official capacity—both secure and disinterested. And these were essential ingredients for an individual as high-spirited as Field.

It was Melvin Gray, after all, who relinquished the sum of money in 1872 and 1873 which permitted Field's flight to Europe, only later to tighten the purse strings to bring him home again. With Gray's assistance, Field, at age twenty-one, came into the majority of his inheritance, which he quickly spent during an elaborate European tour in which he played host to his college companion and future brother-in-law, Edgar V. Comstock. In spite of repeated pleas to Melvin Gray for additional funds, the two sojourners—after traveling through Ireland, England, and France—were met with Gray's shockingly terse cable in Naples, "No funds available."

For Field, however, the message could not be too dismaying. Just before leaving for Europe, he had met Edgar Comstock's sister, Julia, with whom he had fallen in love. He had asked her to marry him immediately if possible, but otherwise *after* his return from Europe, for first he would "round out" his education. Although Field wrote Julia at the beginning of his tour that he expected "to study very diligently and make good progress," he later told a friend that "I just swatted the money around. I had money. I paid it out for experience—it was plenty. Experience was lying around loose."

Like Mark Twain, who had toured Europe in 1869 before settling down to marry Olivia Langdon, Field was continually both fascinated and embarrassed by the contrasts in American and European cultures. He wrote Julia's father:

3 ⧸⧹ *Youth: Homes and Houses*

> The English . . . appear to set themselves up as the lords
> of Creation, as if the little isle of England were in any way better
> than other little isles. Not so with the American. He is all smiles
> to everyone, free with his money, into everything, friendly with
> even the garcons and porters. I can't say that I approve of this
> miscellaneous friendliness but it is perfectly characteristic of the
> American abroad.

When Field returned from Europe, he not only had a better
idea of what constituted an American; he had a better idea of what
his own needs were. Prior to leaving, Field had written Julia
about the loss of his real family and his desires to contact them
through spiritualism. "So am I an orphan," he wrote Julia, "if
I could only see the faces of my father and mother and hold conversation with them, I should be much profited thereby." When
he returned from Europe in 1873, he was still an orphan, still
seeking his lost parents, but, in a sense, he was no longer so in-
tent on trying to regain what in no way could be regained. He
was ready to start forming his own family, or, in any case, to
marry a woman who would be willing to provide the warm, secure household denied him as a youngster. Within the next twenty
years, Julia would give birth to eight children, three of whom (including the Fields' first-born son) would die while still young and
six of whom would be born within the first decade of their married
life. By the time Field moved to Chicago in 1883—exactly ten
years after his marriage to Julia—his family would consist of
four rambunctious children. The eldest, Mary French or "Trotty"
as she was called, provided Julia with the main support for her
servantless house. Then there was Melvin—just two and a half
years Trotty's junior—followed by Eugene, Jr. (nicknamed

"Pinny" after the comic opera *Pinafore*) and Frederick, who Field endearingly referred to as "Daisy" after the popular song "Oh My! Ain't He a Daisy?." No doubt fortunately for Julia, in terms of her domestic burdens, the Fields waited another full decade after arriving in Chicago before further expanding their family. Then, in 1893 and 1894, two additional children were born. Roswell Francis arrived in the spring of 1893 and was immediately dubbed "Posey" or, more kindly, "Pody" or "Po" by his father. And a year later, Ruth Gray, or "Sister Girl," was born.

Julia, even if she had wished, could hardly have avoided her child-rearing responsibilities. But even then, there was an additional child, which, in all likelihood, she had not originally counted on. This "child"—hailed as the nation's "child amongst children" —was Eugene Field.

On the occasion of their eighth wedding anniversary, in 1881, Field wrote his wife, "You have had a hard time, Julia. You loved and married a boy. You were the mother of a boy's children. You are the mother of a big, foolish and yet affectionate boy's children today." In writing this, Field was most serious. But for Julia, if her motherly tasks were not easy, they were made at least somewhat more bearable by Field's continual tributes in verse and prose which he provided for his readers' enjoyment and which, with the passing of the years, came to provide a mainstay of his popular reputation. One such poem, "Lizzie and the Baby," is particularly enlightening in its poetic portrayal of a husband's dual attractions to his wife and "mother." The husband, in this case, has taken his wife, Lizzie, to the concert where she has spent the night "wonderin' ef the baby cried." In the last stanza, the husband reflects:

And nex' to bein' what I be—
    The husband uv my gentle bride—
I'd wisht I wuz that croodlin' wee,
    With Lizzie wonderin' ef I cried.

When Field arrived in Denver, in 1881, where he worked as managing editor of the Denver *Tribune,* he explicitly spelled out Julia's wifely duties:

> I am not going to rent a house till you tell me to do so. Hereafter you must run all the family affairs and you are to run me, too, if you want to! You are a woman now, a wife—a precious wife—and a dear, good mother, and you shall be supreme monarch in your household from this date forward.

The house that Field did finally rent, and the one which Julia did, indeed, "run," was the little house on Colfax—saved by the "Unsinkable" Molly Brown in 1927 and later made into a branch library by the city of Denver. And the sort of family life which Field insisted upon in his letter to Julia was, in fact, the same kind which he humorously described in *The House* in 1895. The opening paragraph of this book begins:

> It was either Plato the Athenian, or Confucius the Chinese, or Andromachus the Cretan—or some other philosopher whose name I disremember—that remarked once upon a time that no woman was happy until she got herself a home. It makes no difference who first uttered this truth, the truth itself is and always has been recognized as one possessing nearly all the virtues of an axiom.

The axiom, of course, might be equally well applied to Field. There can be little doubt that no matter who derived the greater benefits, the responsibility for securing and maintaining the house, in Field's opinion, rested upon the wife's shoulders. In *The House* it was Alice who first expressed the wish that we "might be able to build a dear little house for ourselves"; who hoped that this house might be located in the suburbs amongst "the pure air and the wholesome freedom of rural life"; and who, in spite of all obstacles, finally purchased the house in her name with all "circum-adjacent real estate" belonging not to Reuben "but to Alice and to her heirs and assigns forever."

Although the fictionalized account was obviously exaggerated, it was still the kind of home which Field and a great many men of his generation desired. Like the house the Grays had provided, it was both disinterested and, at the same time, secure in its refuge from temptation, care, and vexation.

As Reuben Baker's neighbor, Mr. Teddy, remarked upon visiting the home, "Your life amid these picturesque environments in this sequestered spot, far from the din and turmoil of the urban throng, will be in every respect ideal—a dream, sir, a poetic dream." He then added that, "the serpent of worldly solicitude, sir, should never be suffered to enter this veritable Eden." Of course, as Reuben was continually to discover, the dream was, indeed, for the most part, "poetic." But, in any case, the popularity of *The House* when it appeared in both the "Sharps and Flats" columns and later in book form was due, in no small measure, to the fact that it so accurately reflected the yearnings of the times.

The November 1895 issue of the *Ladies' Home Journal*— which boasted "a larger circulation than any periodical in the world"—contained a featured article by the Rev. Charles M. Parkhurst on "The Father's Domestic Headship." This headship, according to Dr. Parkhurst, should not make the error of violating the God-given roles of the sexes. "Sex is limitation," warned Dr. Parkhurst, "and to proceed as though it were not has debilitated the manliness of some men and ruined the womanliness of a good many women." This was to say in so many words that the father's "domestic headship" should consist of serving as a "connection between the home and the great outside world" and that the mother, for her part, should concern herself with the "peace of the household and the successful running of its machinery."

Similarly, an article in the November 1895 issue of the *North American Review* entitled "What Becomes of College Women," suggested that women might, indeed, go to college but that the fruits of these labors would be best employed by "bringing the best offering of herself to the worthiest shrine"—the home. The author noted that amongst roles of women graduates were names which "suggest erudite thinking in the mathematics" and whose high stature rested upon their application of this knowledge "to the problems of practical house-keeping. They and their work," noted the author, "represent the high water-mark of our civilization."

Furthermore, if educated women did not apply their learning to the "practical problems" of housekeeping, there was sufficient evidence to indicate the predictable and unfortunate results. An unsigned cartoon in the November 3, 1895 issue of the New York *Times* was entitled, forthrightly, "The Effect of College Education on a Woman's Chances of Marriage," and subtitled "A Little Learning is a Dangerous Thing." As portrayed in this cartoon, the college girl, at age forty, had only 51.8 per cent chance of being married, and was graphically shown with a scrawny cat, a canary, and a stack of ominous-looking books. Her "Society Sister," on the other hand, at age forty had 87.2 per cent chance of being married, and was happily pictured entering her home with the assistance of her liveried porter.

The "society sisters" were obviously women who, in spite of all temptations, had not violated their God-given sex role. As Dr. Parkhurst pointed out, for women there were "infinite stretches of opportunity in the line of service which the general instinct and the revealed word of God shows to be primarily pertinent to her."

Surely, a large part of Field's popularity stemmed from the combined impression of both his personal family life and his poetry and prose, seemingly a hearty confirmation of the proper roles of husband, wife, and family. One form of Field's "domestic headship" was his poetry, so obviously designed to soothe, and provide a safe, poetic reward to the mother's domestic labors. In "Child and Mother" he wrote:

> O Mother-my-love, if you'll give me your hand,
>   And go where I ask you to wander,
> I will lead you away to a beautiful land—
>   The Dreamland that's waiting out yonder.
>
> There'll be no little tired-out boy to undress,
>   No questions or cares to perplex you;
> There'll be no little bruises or bumps to caress,
>   Nor patching of stockings to vex you.
>
> For I'll rock you away on a silver-dew stream,
>   And sing you asleep when you're weary,
> And no one shall know of our beautiful dream
>   But you and your own little dearie.

3   *Youth: Homes and Houses*

Field as the poet of childhood and the versifier of domestic scenes was viewed by many as the ideal husband and provider. It was as if his own peripatetic questings for home and family were later manifested, by means of his writings and personal life, to serve the needs of his readers. In this way he was, in a manner of speaking, the mythic American.

As Hildegarde Hawthorne wrote in *St. Nicholas* Magazine:

> Somehow Field always appears to me as the ideal of the American type. He drew from New England, and was brought up there as a boy, and yet he belonged to the West, which he passionately loved. He loved home folks and home ways as a man loves what is close and dear.

Through his writings, Field's name became synonymous with the "domestic headship" of the nation; he exemplified, in a word, Dr. Parkhurst's essential "connection between the home and the great outside world."

Charles Scribner's Sons

Field's father, Roswell Martin Field, received fame for his courtroom defense of Dred Scott but had little time for his sons.

Denver Public Library

Despite his mother's early death, when Field was six, he
would later remember her in poetic tribute. Pictured here,
Field and his mother, Frances Reed Field, *c.* 1851.

Field received the "best of New England influences" after he moved to the home of his cousin, Mary Field French in Amherst.

Denver Public Library

Charles Scribner's Sons

At his grandmother's home in Newfane, Vermont, Field became aware of the "incongruous" ways of the Puritan faith.

Field, age 12.   Field, age 18.   Field, age 19.

Denver Public Library

Denver Public Library

At the University of Missouri, Field displayed his penchant for practical jokery by dressing in a colorful skirt and singing "Old Aunt Jemima, Oh, High, Oh."

The Eugene Field House

In marrying Julia Comstock, Field found a woman who was willing to provide the warm, secure household denied him as a youngster. Pictured here, Field and Julia on their wedding trip, 1873.

Mrs. Eugene Field

Mary French (Trotty)
—born March 5, 1876

Eugene Jr. (Pinny)
—born January 28, 1880

Roswell Francis
(Po, Posy, Pody)
—born March 27, 1893

Ruth Gray (Sister Girl)
—born March 27, 1894

Ruth and
Frederick Comstock (Daisy)
—born September 3, 1881

Posy

Posy and Ruth

Chicago Historical Society

Posy

Denver:
Platitudes and Pressures

In the years following Field's death—and despite all efforts to the contrary—comments occasionally arose seriously challenging the national status of Field's "domestic headship." In 1901, when Slason Thompson brought out his highly complimentary biography of his friend and associate, he hinted that there might be a neglected, and perhaps unpleasant, aspect to the character of the nation's "Children's Laureate." These remarks, however brief, cast an indelible shadow on Field's posthumous reputation. In fact, no biographer after Thompson could avoid the difficult subject entirely.

As Thompson had so tersely put it in 1901, "Field's fondness for other people's children was like that of an entomologist for bugs—for purposes of study, dissection, and classification." In so opening the floodgates of contention, Thompson obviously intended little harm. He prefaced his remarks by quoting from Field's own written legacy—his brief "Auto-Analysis" which, as

Field had put it in 1894, contained "facts, confessions, and observations for the information of those who, for one reason or another, are applying to me for biographical data concerning myself."

Thompson, while seeing this piece as basically a combination of half-truths and whimsical observations—"My favorite color is red," "I am very fond of dogs, birds and all small pets," and so forth—quoted Field as confessing that he "did not love all children." And then added his own surprising belief that no matter what else was contained in the "Auto-Analysis," that this statement—that Field did not love all children—comprised Field's "truest words." In Thompson's view it was easy to see why, in 1894, Field's comments had been accepted with such overwhelming incredulity. Field's audience had, after all, based most of their conceptions of the poet's love for children on the sentiments contained in his lullabies, his "Little Boy Blue," and his "Wynken, Blynken and Nod." Yet, based on his own personal experience with Field, Thompson recalled that Field not only did "not love all children, he truly loved very few children." Specifically, remembered Thompson, he loved only his own children. The most serious outcry against Thompson came from Julia. For her, the book was utterly unacceptable, partly because of Thompson's remarks about Field's relationships with children and partly because he suggested that Field, at times, both drank and smoked. Ultimately, because of Thompson's alleged "indiscretions," Julia was able to convince the editors at Scribners to withdraw *Heredity and Contradictions* from publication.

Yet, despite such efforts, or perhaps to some degree because of them, the argument that Field "did not love all children" could not be quashed. One reason was the caustic and well-published review of *Heredity and Contradictions* by William Marion Reedy of the St. Louis *Sunday Mirror*. In Reedy's view, Thompson's continuously worshipful attitude toward Field combined both the "affectionateness and a great deal of the stupidity of Boswell." But nonetheless, added Reedy, "this biographer tells us one truth that is important to Field's fame and that is, that he never cared for children generally." Reedy continued to note that Field's "devotion to children was, to a great extent a pose. It was a good pose, an effective pose. And that is all it was." Reedy did not object to naming "schools after him, if we will, but let us not continue to fool the people by picturing him to them as a sort of Sunday-school seraph."

Reedy's caustic opinions, of course, stood in direct opposition to those of most reviewers who merely took the opportunity of Thompson's biography to inflate still further the growing reputation of Eugene Field. For Field's preservationists, even the slightest blemish on Field's record could not be tolerated. Other biographers would continually quibble over the veracity of Thompson's remarks. Writers such as Melville Stone, while steadfastly denying that Field was inherently evil, did recall that if there was a child near Field in the theater, he had a habit of turning and making a face, which would set the infant bawling. And in 1924, Charles Dennis attempted to clear up the matter once and for all, by declaring that:

> My long friendship with both Thompson and Stone, which extends over more than forty years, convinces me that the words of theirs were based on hearsay evidence, though both were intimately associated with Field. Surely neither of them would have permitted Field or any one else deliberately to frighten a little child in his presence without first administering to the offender

such a rebuke as would have deterred him from repeating the offence.

"For my own part," added Dennis, "I can testify that I never saw Field conduct himself in the presence of children otherwise than in a manner to gladden their little hearts."

The confusion amongst Field's friends regarding his relationships with children was compounded by the peculiar evidence generally supporting Reedy's opinion of the author's early, humorous verse. William Marion Reedy, in his review, saw this untempered writing as the product of the "real" Field which belied the calculated sentimentality of his later writing. In Reedy's words:

> The Field that people have overdone as an idol came into being chiefly through his cute discovery that the way to reach the public most effectively was through sentiment and not through humor. He set to work deliberately to cultivate the sentimental and he did so with what success the whole world knows. That [these writings] are such a *tour de force* into sentiment by such a rank unsentimentalist, a congenital and cultivated unsentimentalist, is their chiefest claim to attention.

Reedy's essentially moralistic sense of betrayal by Field no doubt stemmed in part from the fact that both he and Field had been St. Louis newspapermen for at least a part of their lives. And though many of Field's early colleagues looked upon the rise of his reputation more fondly than Reedy, surely, even the most charitable could not fail to note the increasing discrepancy between the resurrected deity and the early reporter.

Nearly thirty years before Reedy attacked what he termed the "Eugene Field Myth," Field had begun his writing career in

St. Louis. Returning penniless from Europe in 1873 to marry
Julia, Field had found himself obliged to work as a reporter for
the St. Louis *Journal*. And so, for the next ten years of his career—including the time Field spent as managing editor of the
Denver *Tribune* (1881–1883) and his two brief stints on the St.
Joseph *Gazette* (1875–1876) and the Kansas City *Times* (1880)
—there would be little in Field's written record which would indicate his eventual metamorphosis into the nation's "Children's
Laureate." The bulk of this production, in fact, would indicate
the exact opposite. Slason Thompson termed these years the "hob-
bledehoy period of his literary career," and Charles Dennis in an
attempt to avoid serious discussion of these years altogether, titled
his book *Eugene Field's Creative Years* and focused on Field's
experiences *after* he settled down in Chicago.

Surely much of what Reedy, on the one hand, saw as Field's
congenital unsentimentality and what Thompson and Dennis, on
the other, passed off as Field's youthful prankishness, was, in truth,
a very honest reaction on Field's part to the confrontation of the
ideals of his New England upbringing with the realities of an ur-
banizing frontier. In a sardonic paragraph he wrote for the Denver
Tribune, Field complained:

> Mamma is Larruping Papa with the Mop Handle. The Chil-
> dren are Fighting over a Piece of Pie in the Kitchen. Over the
> Piano there is a Beautiful Motto in a gilt Frame. The Beautiful
> Motto says there is no Place like Home.

It is doubtful that at this point in Field's career—or, for that
matter any other point—he was threatened with Julia's "larruping"
mop handle. Rather, his comments seem more to embody his frus-

trations with a society steeped in the hypocrisy of easy platitudes—the same platitudes which had, in fact, influenced his New England childhood and continued to plague him throughout his college experience.

In Denver, where the bulk of Field's unsentimental verse was written, one can most clearly see the emerging social values which so provoked his rebellious pen. In 1881, upon Field's arrival, Denver was revelling in the ostentatious profits of an exuberant economy. Unchecked optimism pervaded much of the city's commercial sector, resulting in greatly inflated accounts of the city's social and cultural status. As one enthusiastic visitor proclaimed, "Denver becomes to Colorado what Paris is to France." He then further explained that because of the unprecedented profits from Denver's industries, that citizens were now providing the "amenities of intellectual culture that make life so attractive in the old-established centers of civilization where selected society, thoughtful study, and the riches of art, have ripened to maturity through long time and under gracious traditions."

As managing editor of the Denver *Tribune,* Field was capable of knowing the utter folly of such remarks. In truth, the *Tribune,* as well as virtually all other large enterprises concerned with the "amenities" of Denver's cultural life, were controlled to one extent or another by the mammoth Denver and Rio Grande Railroad. As Slason Thompson pointed out about the *Tribune,* it "was run on a scale of extravagance . . . its newspaper functions being altogether subordinate to its services as a railroad ally and political organ." And, in a perhaps somewhat different but nonetheless apt use of the word "extravagant," Field wrote Julia on September 25, 1881, that "without you . . . before my eyes I am tempted into many extravagancies. The *Tribune* set are the most extravagant people I have ever become associated with." These "extravagancies" were, of course, oft-times in the form of plentiful material goods which could easily be used either as out-and-out bribes or merely—by the fact of their ubiquitous presence—to influence editorial discretion. An article in the *Tribune,* dated the same day as Field's letter to Julia, was entitled "The Passion for Diamonds." In it, the question was put to the unidentified "authority": "Are there more diamonds worn now than ever before in this country?" And the unhesitating response: "I should say so, most decidedly. I have been in the business over thirty years, and I never knew such a rage for the stone as exists today." And similarly, it is no small wonder that, in the paragraph Field addressed to his alleged child readers of the *Tribune,* he made mention of the much-coveted gem.

> The man on the Sidewalk is a Jeweler. The Editor Owes him Eight Thousand dollars for Diamonds. That is Why the Editor sneaks down the Alley instead of Meeting the Jeweler. Would you like to be an Editor and Sneak down an Alley?

The dilemma of possessing unpaid-for diamonds, of course, could not be taken as directed solely at Field's young readers. It was also a question which Field, himself, must have been grappling with at the time.

In a society where one's financial rewards were more often than not dictated by the politics of mining or railroad opportunists, how did one gauge his real worth either as a newspaperman or a private citizen? What could be considered the proper role of one's "domestic headship" in a land where one's very job necessitated the constant mingling with men of "extravagant ways"? Similarly, how did one play the role of gentleman or lady among men or women who had no formal education? Or, perhaps more to the point, how did one bring up children on the "touchstones" of British or New England classics in a frontier city where vernacular was the only tongue?

Not surprisingly, in writing his paragraphs for the Denver *Tribune,* Field often picked for a model that enduring symbol of his own educational background—the *New England Primer.* From this book Field derived the title for his first bound volume of paragraphs (*The Tribune Primer*) and, in so doing, selected such appropriate subheadings as "Tales Designed for the Information and Edification of the Nursery Brigade" and "Pretty Stories for the Pleasure and Profit of Little Children." That Field played some peculiar and ironic reversals on the original text, however, may be gathered from the following:

> The Apple is in a Basket. A Worm is in the Apple. It is a juicy little white Worm. Suppose you Eat the Apple, where will the Worm be?

Or, to illustrate the same motif in a different context and form:

> A stands for Apples, so hard and so Green—
> B stands for Boy who is going away—
> C stands for Colic that Soon will be seen—
> D stands for Devil that's shortly to pay.

Whether or not the *New England Primer* was directly employed in Field's early training, the influence of this Calvinist text must have borne its strong imprint on his memory. After all, in his grandmother's interpretation of her *duties* to "God and mankind," her "Puritan" faith had been most apparent. And once Field had sufficiently freed himself from his New England heritage, and realized that the neatly patterned models of life offered in the *Primer* bore little relationship to the manner of one's later life, he felt equally free, if not compelled, to expose the absurdities he found around him.

These absurdities often were perpetrated by those seeking, for one reason or another, to boost Denver's cultural image. One such perpetrator was Ernest Ingersoll, who, in 1885, wrote *Crest of the Continent: A Summer's Ramble in the Rocky Mountains and Beyond.* The uniqueness of Denver, according to Ingersoll, evolved around the civilized state of her community life. In Ingersoll's words:

> So, out of the barrenness of the cactus-plain has arisen a cultivated and beautiful city of 75,000 people, which is truly a metropolis. On each side of every street flows a constant stream of water, often as clear and cool as a mountain brook. After dinner (for Denver dines at five o'clock as a rule), the father of the house lights his cigar and turns hoseman for an hour, while he chats with friends. The swish and gurgle and sparkle of water are always present, and always must be; for so Denver defies the desert and dissipates the dreaded dust.

As the "father of the house" and one familiar with Denver's rapidly changing climate, Field was well aware that the "gurgle and sparkle" of water were not the only things which occupied his leisure-time attention. In 1881, Field wrote Julia, "One thing that will worry you mightily about Denver life is the ditches that run along the sides of the streets. They will be a source of constant delight to the children and I can easily fancy Pinny and Melvin wading up to their waist in them." Field, logically enough, gave the following mutinous advice to the loyal fans of his "nursery brigade":

> What a Delightful Mud Hole! It is quite Deep and Inviting. How Cool and Pleasant it must be in the Mud Hole. Good little Boys and Girls can Play in the Mud Hole and Make Lots of Nice Patty Cakes. Tell the Baby to Come, too, and then you can Put Mud in his Ears and he will Splash the pretty Black Water all over Susie's new Frock.

And, in the issue of the Denver *Tribune* dated the same date as Field's letter to Julia in 1881, an editorial warned that "the sidewalk question has been pretty well discussed, yet at the present rate of progress many years will elapse before even the principal thoroughfares will be made passable in muddy weather."

Fashionable ladies in Denver in the 1880's were continually subjected to appeals to dress in a manner utterly inappropriate for the local conditions. Promotions such as the front-page ad for Charles Ballin & Co. advised potential shoppers that "walking through their store no lady could help declaring, 'Oh! how elegant.'" And continued to point out for the hard-to-convince that "Nothing finer can be seen in New York City."

In the face of such deceptive attractions, Field suggested such realistic heresies in the *Tribune* as:

> The Mud is in the Street. The Lady has on a pair of Red Stockings. She is trying to Cross the Street. Let us all give Three cheers for the Mud.

Similarly, any misconceptions about romantic love were soon dashed by Field's caustic pen. What point was there in adhering to conventions of romantic love in a land which continually mocked such codes, where women oft-times spoke a language more appropriate to miners than to gentry. Where a woman might, in one instance, tell her lover "Oh, yes, you do look awful cute!" in regard to his courting attire and, then, turn around to apply the same language to a passing donkey. ("I quote her language with a sigh / 'Oh, Charlie, ain't he awful cute?'"). Or, in another instance, one's romantic notions might be quickly dampened by the lover's unexpectedly candid response. In "The Dimple," the girl is heard to reply:

> You may kiss, since your kisses I loftily prize,
> This cute little mole on my cheek.
> What you think is a dimple, I pray you be calm,
> Is an old vaccination scar deep in my arm,
>   Be calm!
> It's an old vaccination you see on my arm!

When Ernest Ingersoll had visited Denver in the 1880's he had been duly impressed with the elegant new houses which graced Denver's "water-lined" streets. "Homes succeed one another in endlessly varying styles of architecture . . . with porches well occupied during the long, cool twilight . . . giving a very attractive air of opulence and ease." Field, however, who was then living in his cramped little house on West Colfax, was not so easily deceived by the façades of opulence and ease. He knew that if inside Mamma was not "Larruping Papa with the Mop Handle," there might be similar, equally disastrous, episodes going on. Cockroaches, mice, and other insects and rodents were a continual source of harassment to even the best-run households. If Denver women, on the one hand, were encouraged to bake golden cakes, delicately browned bread, and quivering jellies because "material things glorified for the good of one's dear ones are fit expressions of any woman," Field also realized that there were serious obstacles to these tasks. Even in homes with servants, a mouse could conceivably fall into the flour barrel. "The Cook baked him in a Loaf of Bread, and here he lies on the Table cut in two by the Sharp bread Knife. But," added Field mischievously, "we will not Eat poor Mouse. We will eat the Bread, but we will Take the Mousie and Put him in the Cistern." And, in a perhaps equally mischievous mood, Field advised, in the case of finding a cockroach crawling across one's pillow, to "lie still and Keep your Mouth open. He will crawl into your Mouth and You can Bite him in Two. This will Teach him to be more Discreet in the Future."

Occasionally, the houses of Field's darker imagination were found to be plagued with problems more serious than household pests. Such was the case of Susie and Charlie whose penchant for violence at first glance seemingly reflects on the Puritan child's "instinct for destruction."

> This is a gun. Is the Gun Loaded? I do not know. Let us Find out. Put the Gun on the table, and you, Susie, blow down one barrel, while you, Charlie, blow down the other. Bang! Yes, it was loaded. Run quick Jennie, and pick up Susie's head and Charlie's lower Jaw before the Nasty Blood gets over the New carpet.

Field's main point, however, does not seem to be so much concerned with the inherent evil of little children as, again, the sort of society which allowed guns to lie around freely and the society which permitted the outward decorum of the house to dictate the lives within. In such a society, how could one establish a wholesome family life? For Field, a viable solution seemed to lie only in the untainted sensibilities of the young. As he had written Lillie Olmstead in 1869, regarding the development of the child, "It is, then, when the little one begins to reason, that it begins actually to sin! So it was with our 'General Parent'—at first having a child's mental faculties—he finally developed into a being with the mind and dispositions of a man! The Serpent was the faculty of Reason!'"

Though Field obviously changed his views somewhat by the time he reached Denver, his basic philosophy apparently remained the same—at least with regard to the detrimental effects of Reason on the child's purity. In Denver, Field's modified position seemed to hold that the child's most corrupting influence came from a society which "educated" children by merely imbuing them with the illusory standards of the larger society. It was the act committed *against* the child by the adult world—the actual offering of the apple, so to speak—which, in Field's view, served to corrupt the child's innate sensibilities.

Field, in a more literary mood, once praised the child's God-gift, fancy. "This gift," declared Field, "first manifests itself in the trait which is vulgarly called lying, and all children have it to a degree. It is a beautiful inheritance; it may develop into an evil habit or it may redound gloriously to the advantage of humanity." In the paragraphs Field wrote for the Denver *Tribune,* he appeared to endorse a kind of "fancy" which many would not hesitate to call lying or worse.

> The old Man is Blind and cannot See. He holds his Hat in his Hand and there is a Dime in the Hat. Go up quietly and Take the Dime out of the Hat. The Man cannot See you. Next Sunday

you can put the Dime in the Sabbath School box and the Teacher will Praise you. Your Papa will put some Money in the Contribution box, too. He will put More in than you do. But his Opportunities for Robbing are better than yours.

When Field arrived in Denver, the educational institutions—in the form of schools and churches—had already organized themselves into large operations for dispensing packaged morality. By 1889, in fact, Denver boasted sixty-two churches for a population of about 100,000 and a Y.M.C.A. with the highest membership (over 1,200) of any similar-sized city in the world. It was reported that "the religious meetings of the Association are all largely attended by young men, and on Sunday afternoons many have been turned away for want of room." Similarly, the effectiveness of Denver's school system was discussed with untempered patriotic fervor. One such account reported that "the superintendents and principals are the skilled generals of the educational army, which has nowhere its superior. The work is so cleverly systematized, the wheels of the machinery and the results are so excellent, that the public does not always stop to consider the immense force which must be brought to bear by officers and teachers."

As Field must have well realized from his own upbringing, the child who was forced to learn from such a system had either to yield passively to the adult authorities or else, as Field did himself, rebel. Much of Field's Denver verse contains a sense of the defiant spirit which had caused his premature dismissal from Williams and his near-dismissal from both Knox and the University of Missouri:

How many Birds are there in Seven soft-boiled Eggs?
If you have Five Cucumbers and eat Three, what will you

have left? Two? No, you are Wrong. You will have more than that.
You will have Colic enough to Double you up in a Bow Knot for
Six Hours. You may go to the Foot of the Class.

Field, in his *Tribune* sketches, deplored the methods in school,
church, and home which insisted upon filling children with mun-
dane facts while turning them into priggish, pretentious adults.
He wrote about his own education: "I think that a grievous mis-
take was made in putting me at my studies so early. Setting
me at Latin at seven years of age was simply a crime!" And so
far as his own children were concerned, a friend who remembered
them during Field's Denver years recalled, "they were wild little
things. Their father used to frolic with them much of the time and
allowed them the freedom that made them so intense in their play."

In his newspaper paragraphs, Field's advice to the young members of his "Nursery Brigade" included such insurrectionary acts
against the proper decorum of school and home as placing a bent
pin on the teacher's chair so "it will Bite the School Teacher," or,
defacing the walls by painting them with ink or mashing the "Nice
yellow Custard" of a caterpillar on them.

Perhaps, then, William Marion Reedy had been right when,
in 1901, he had advised parents either to stop naming schools after
Field or else be aware that Field was not a "Sunday-school seraph."
But he had been mistaken in implying that because Field's early
verse was unsentimental that this somehow supported Thompson's
contention that Field "did not love all children." In fact, disre-
garding Field's personal attitude toward children, his early writing offered nothing less than a manifesto for liberating the child
from a stultifying social and educational environment.

The schools, however, in resurrecting Field's memory paid
scant attention to his early verses. As members of the educational

army, they were obviously more interested in promoting a desired behavior than encouraging anything as insurrectionary as the "God-gift, fancy." As the preface wistfully noted in *Common-School Literature* (which contained Field's "Little Boy Blue" and "Singing in God's Acre"), "Every beautiful sentiment implanted in the fertile mind of youth is a seed-truth that will yield a perennial harvest of good thought developed into worthy acts." Or, as the more unabashedly patriotic preface to *Literature of America and Our Favorite Authors* declared, "The first and main purpose of the work is to present to our American homes a mass of wholesome, varied and well-selected reading matter. These homes are the schools of citizenship, and—next to the Bible, which is the foundation of our morals and laws—we need those books which at once entertain and instruct, and, at the same time, stimulate patriotism and pride for our native land."

Within a few years after his death, Field's poetry had become a standard offering for schools across the country. As William Marion Reedy regretfully pointed out in 1901, "nearly every city of any importance contains a public school named after Eugene Field." Moreover, "Eugene Field Days" became a common occurrence in classrooms both at home and abroad. Mary E. Burt, in her preface to *The Eugene Field Book,* which was explicitly intended for classroom use, recalled that as early as 1885 she had first been impressed with the value of Eugene Field while visiting schools in Liverpool, England. There, she had witnessed "about a hundred boys, of an average age of ten or eleven years, reciting 'The Rock-a-By Lady' with great spirit. . . . I was reassured," wrote Mary Burt, "that a new poet had come to share the laurels so generously bestowed by the American public on Whittier, Longfellow, Lowell, and Holmes."

The Field fever, however, apparently reached its peak in America some years later. Grace Faxon, as an associate editor of *Normal Instructor and Primary Plans,* reported that the greatest demand for Field material came into her office during the years 1893 to 1910. Her own fondness for Field in the classroom was based on personal experience. "Before I entered literary work," noted Miss Faxon, "I taught in the public schools of Massachusetts. I know that there has always been a great interest in Field among teachers. It was a very common thing to have a 'Field Afternoon.'" She then added that she could not "say definitely that there has been any school board who authorized a Field Afternoon but I feel sure that many have recommended it."

Indeed, not only a school board but an entire state system had endorsed a "Eugene Field Day." By 1897, schools throughout Missouri, on the recommendation of the State Superintendent of Public Schools, observed annually the date of Field's death with "suitable programs made up from the dead poet's writings and articles eulogistic of him and his works."

The poems selected for classroom use were generally either those poems of Field's later, and safer, fancy, such as "The Sugar-Plum Tree," "The Duel," or "Wynken, Blynken and Nod," or else those which told of the child's innocent dying, such as "Little Boy Blue" or "The Singing in God's Acre." The occasion of the death of a child was used in the classroom as an opportunity to contemplate one's own transgressions and to promote good behavior on earth. The customary pattern of instruction in the turn-of-the-century schoolbooks was to provide after each story or poem "a little dictionary which has in it all the words that can give you [the child reader] any trouble. This will tell you how to pronounce the words and what they mean. Study this and be sure you know exactly how to use each word." As Frank Cooley, the superintendent of schools in Evansville, Indiana, instructed teachers in his introduction to *The Eugene Field Reader,* the important thing was not that the child should be able to read the poem itself, but rather "the child should be encouraged to find the familiar words in it." Such instructional lists, when employed with "Little Boy Blue," ran the gamut from those containing words like "little," and "boy," and "blue" (as in *The Eugene Field Reader*), to more challenging lists such as those selected by Frances and Andrew Blodgett in their *Second Reader.* There can be little doubt about the impact on the young mind of lists of the latter category which emphasized more difficult words, like "rust," "toddling," "faithful," "awaiting," and "molds."

In resuscitating Field's memory for America's young, the authors of the schoolroom texts had few qualms about emphasizing the facts of Field's upbringing which they felt would shed the most light on the desired message. Mildred Rutherford in her *American Literature,* while failing to note that Field's father was an avowed agnostic, pointed out that Field's mother was a "Southern woman" and a Christian who taught her children to pray. "She instilled into her boy a love for God and a love for God's little ones, and Eugene Field strove to teach as he was taught." A similar instructional tone is caught in Clara Banta's discussion of Field's poem about his Amherst dog "Dooley," about whom Field once wrote:

> Oh, had I wings like a dove I would fly
> Away from this world of fleas!
> I'd fly all round Miss Emerson's yard
> And light on Miss Emerson's trees.

Here, emphasis is placed on Field's "pity for this pet suffering from heat and fleas." And while failing to point out that among Field's renowned practical jokes were those which involved painting a horse and catching goldfish from a bowl beside his bed, Miss Banta merely notes that "it shows us what a kind-hearted little fellow he was. A boy who loves animals and treats them kindly never grows up to be a bad man." Nor, of course, as might be expected, is there latitude in Miss Banta's explanation for inclusion of Field's own advice from the *Tribune Primer,* such as:

> The Cat is Asleep on the Rug. Step on her Tail and See if she will Wake up. Oh, no; She will not wake. She is a heavy Sleeper. Perhaps if you Were to saw her Tail off with the Carving knife you might Attract her attention. Suppose you try.

As generations of America's children grew to adulthood, there can be little doubt as to the influence of the grade school readers in shaping their notions of Field, and, accordingly, of society at large. By 1900, at a time when Field's poetry was being most widely circulated in the classroom, only 1 per cent of the entire school population ever attained what is commonly called higher education. Only 5 per cent went on to high school and more than half of the nation's school children dropped out before completing fifth grade. In other words, virtually anyone who had any kind of schooling was exposed to the Field of "Little Boy Blue" and "Wynken, Blynken and Nod," while being denied knowledge of Field's verse in the *Tribune Primer.* And if there was an aspect to Field's character which might seem "unsafe" for children—as Thompson had hinted and Reedy had so boldfacedly stated—that aspect had been completely glossed over by the time Field's young readers were old enough to have children of their own. Even Reedy, who had zealously championed the only serious attack on Field's character, later underwent a change of heart. In 1918, he wrote to a friend, "Confidentially, although everything I wrote in that pamphlet was true, I often wish now that I hadn't written it. I'm firmly convinced that we need myths to get along on by and by."

Denver Public Library

The mammoth Denver and Rio Grand Railroad influenced virtually all aspects of Denver's cultural life during the 1880's.

Denver Public Library

Denver Public Library

Field's Denver *Tribune* office was located in the same building as the Bank of Denver. His editorship necessitated the constant mingling with men of "extravagant" ways.

Young readers of Field's *Tribune* verse were encouraged to "Play in the Mud Hole and Make Lots of Nice Patty Cakes."

Denver Public Library

Denver Public Library

Field was not easily deceived by the facades of opulence and ease which graced Denver's "water-lined" streets.

Denver Public Library

Denver street scene with Tabor Grand Opera House in background, *c.* 1880.

Denver Public Library

The effectiveness of Denver's school system was discussed with untempered patriotic fervor. Pictured here, youngsters with exercise sticks.

Denver Public Library

During their Denver years, Field's children were remembered as "wild little things." Trotty, Melvin, and Pinny, 1883.

1895

Denver Public Library

Field's early writing offered a manifesto for liberating the child from a stultifying social and educational environment. Trotty with cigarette, 1895.

His

Rabelaisian Nature

The problem of unraveling the myth from the man was one which each of Field's friends and biographers confronted individually. In Slason Thompson's biography of 1901, he appeared to side with the myth by stating unequivocally that "it is far from my intention and farther from my friendship to disturb any of the preconceptions that have been formed from the perusal of his [Field's] works." But by 1927, when Thompson revised his earlier work, he took a stance closer to the man by saying that his "rewriting" was necessary because Dennis, in his 1924 biography, had attempted "the impossible task of putting the irrepressible Gene in corsets with an incipient halo." In so doing, Thompson dared what had never before been dared. In a nationally published biography, he included the first four stanzas of Field's "sub rosa" poem, "Little Willie." As Thompson put it at the time:

For thirty years this innocent brother of "Little Boy Blue" has lived a furtive and vagrant existence, denied entrance to the company of its fellows in *Songs of Childhood*, "With Trumpet and Drum," etc., and from that fact giving currency to all sorts of stories of the suppression of "a large body of Fieldian verse that was the exact reverse of pure," as charged by one reviewer of the early biographies.

The particular, unnamed reviewer, as might be expected, was William Marion Reedy, who (in 1901) had completed his remarks about Thompson's book by commenting simply that Field's bawdy verse "was a matter upon which one [could] not well, or safely, say more, even if one wished to do so."

There can be little doubt, however, that Thompson—even in ushering the unfortunate "Little Willie" into the public spotlight in 1927—retained many of Reedy's feelings about the delicacy of the topic. For even at this late date, he cut short the "innocent brother" by one "unmentionable" stanza. Thompson's version of "Little Willie" went as follows:

> When Willie was a little boy,
>   No more than five or six,
> Right constantly he did annoy
>   His mother with his tricks.
> Yet not a picayune cared I
>   For what he did or said,
> Unless, as happened frequently,
>   The rascal wet the bed.
>
> Closely he cuddled up to me,
>   And put his hands in mine,

Till all at once I seemed to be
　　Afloat in seas of brine.
Sabean odors clogged the air,
　　And filled my soul with dread,
Yet I could only grin and bear
　　When Willie wet the bed.

'Tis many times that rascal has
　　Soaked all the bedclothes through,
Whereat I'd feebly light the gas
　　And wonder what to do.
Yet there he lay, so peaceful like;
　　God bless his curly head,
I quite forgave the little tyke
　　For wetting of the bed.

Ah me, those happy days have flown.
　　My boy's a father, too,
And little Willies of his own
　　Do what he used to do.
And I! Ah, all that's left for me
　　Is dreams of pleasure fled!
Our boys ain't what they used to be
　　When Willie wet the bed.

Field's own "Little Willie," however, ended on a somewhat less subtle note:

Had I my choice, no shapely dame
　　Should share my couch with me,
No amorous jade of tarnished fame,
　　Nor wench of high degree;

> But I would choose and choose again
>   The little curly head,
> Who cuddled close beside me when
>   He used to wet the bed.

Although it is conceivable that four stanzas of "Little Willie" were the extent of Thompson's knowledge of Field's "sub rosa," this seems highly unlikely considering his relationship to Field. By 1926, at least nineteen private editions of "Little Willie" had appeared, only five of which had—like Thompson's—the final stanza deleted. Furthermore, as the collector of Field manuscripts, James Shields, recalled, Thompson once "told me in Chicago some years ago of many 'unprintables' handed him by Field in the editorial rooms which Thompson (as one may well believe) pocketed but destroyed immediately on leaving 'Gene's' presence."

What so offended Thompson's sensibilities was not the humorous idea that Field might prefer the "sabean" pleasures of sleeping with "Little Willie" to those of a woman—but rather that this particular woman might perchance be a "shapely dame." Acceptance of this stanza would have meant accepting the notion that a nineteenth-century gentleman—and in this case, the "Children's Laureate"—might contemplate sharing his couch with an "amorous jade of tarnished fame" or a "wench of high degree."

In point of fact, Field had not only conceived such misadventures, but had written of them colorfully and in great detail. Such notorious figures of the Fieldian underground as Lady Lil ("she screwed for keeps / And laid her victims out in heaps") or The Fair Limousin ("There was no form of harlotry, nor any size of tarse, / That had not run the gauntlet 'twixt her nostrils and her arse") were familiar figures at men's club meetings and in private editions from the 1880's on. Gershon Legman, for example, estimated in 1964 that "Our Lady Lil," in its often abbreviated form, remained as "probably the best-known erotic rhymed recitation in America."

Field's bawdy poetry was, for the most part, meant to be read aloud—usually in the exclusive presence of males. As William Seymour of the Sea Serpent Club wrote Field in 1895, "for many summers past one of 'yours' has been enjoyed with the coffee and cigars after dinner." Adding that, "You never sent me 'When Willie Wet the Bed,' by the way, which you promised me when I last saw you in Boston." "Little Willie," perhaps more than "Our Lady Lil" or "The Fair Limousin," became standard fare at such meetings. George Ade recalled being at a dinner party where Field recited "the poem about Willie. I think that dinner was at the Union League Club," remembered Ade, "and that many members of the old *Morning News* or *Record* staff were present. I seem to remember that I received a printed copy of the poem as a souvenir of the occasion." And Francis Wilson—who claimed he would have beat Thompson to the punch in publishing "Little Willie," had not his own publishers "shown the white feather"—recalled in his memoirs that when Field would recite "Little Willie," as he often did, "it never failed to touch the heart of those who were privileged to hear him."

As long, then, as they were not in danger of being indecently exposed to the public, "The Fair Limousin," "Little Willie," and their cohorts were considered safe enough company for their select male admirers. Even "Socratic Love" (which described the homosexual escapades of Socrates) was not considered out of order when presented for the first time before the Papyrus Club of Boston in 1888. According to this "story" of Athenean times, the young

Alcibiades was "such a pink of fashion" as to fill Socrates with "a violent and lewd desire to bugger."

> For weeks and months old Socrates had had a priapism,
> His pond'rous ods, a sight for Gods, were both surcharged with
>   gism.
> Seeing that bum and this first chance, he made up his mind to
>   spot 'em,
> So he hit 'em a lick with his Attic prick, and occupied Alcy's
>   bottom.

In verse such as this, the obvious intention was more to provoke laughter than to titillate. Yet, considering the rough-grained nature of such rhyme, it is somewhat surprising to find Francis Wilson publicly declaring that "He [Field] had no squeamishness, yet I never heard him tell a coarse story." And this was especially remarkable coming from the man whose personal library contained his own prized edition of *Libidinous Facetiae*—including such writings as "And Only a Boy" and "Passionate Mythology," among others. The implication here, however, may not be so much to defame Wilson's honor as to illustrate his abiding sense of loyalty to the good fellowship of the men's club bards. Wilson's reaction upon receiving a copy of "Socratic Love" is typical. He wrote Field, "that manuscript just tickled me to death! Now that *is* a possession. I have a bully lie as to how I came by it and it all reflects to your wife's credit." Field and his fellow devotees of bawdy literature took the greatest precautions when it came to shielding non-initiates—particularly women—from possible contamination.

Field's own sense of protectiveness when it came to his wife's knowledge of "impure" matters was not markedly dissimilar from Mark Twain's attitude toward Olivia Langdon. Where Twain had once written to his wife, "You are as pure as snow, and I would have you always so—untainted, untouched even by the impure thoughts of others," Field wrote to Julia, "I want you to promise me one thing, that when you happen to be with the girls and they get to talking upon private matters, such as the sexual relations of husband and· wife, you will go away and have nothing to hear of such things."

Also like Twain, Field wrote much that was, in end result, as much scatological as sexual in nature. Although Twain's much-discussed *1601* is mild by comparison with a great deal that Field wrote, it is similar in its emphasis on such body-function humor as wind-breaking and fornication. Both derive their puerile humor from placing unlikely figures in compromising situations. Twain set Queen Elizabeth up in her court to discover "the fellow to this fart," and then allowed the various court members to converse on the likely modes and manners of the participants ("I built a conversation which *could* have happened—I used words such as were used at that time—1601"). Field, in a variant vein, relied on the precedent set by Robert Herrick for his "In Imitation of Robert Herrick on Julia Unlacing Herself."

> But when my Julia breaks her wind,
>   There issues from her fair behind
> A breath that would become, I ween,
>   A Pallas or a Paphian Queen;
>
> No hollow clamor speaks the birth
>   Of this etherial child of earth,
> But hot and swift it mounts the air,
>   Dispensing savour everywhere;
> Swooning with ecstacy, I kiss
>   The heaven that breathed this gale of bliss.

Although there can be no mistaking the similarity in names between Herrick's subject and Field's wife, the object does not seem so much intended to disparage Julia, as to employ Herrick's original character while again playing upon the incongruities of a society which set women on immaculate pedestals where bodily functions were either ignored or denied existence altogether.

Sometimes Field's "sub rosa" poems were merely the adaptations for male audiences of concepts which occurred in his newspaper verse designed for both sexes and of various stations in society. In writing of a "Summer Complaint" for the St. Louis *Times-Journal,* Field envisioned an idyllic life of the ancient deities away from the city's swelter.

> Imagine Cupid at his play,
> For boys will play when out of school—
> Imagine Juno keeping cool
> With palm-leaf fan and white pekay.
>
> Imagine Vulcan come from work,
> Where anvils ring and forges glare—
> Imagine Venus' languid air,
> Her welcome voice and loving smirk.

This idyllic life, however, when adapted to the sexual humors of Field's male audience is provided with the same figures—but in a more sportive climate. In his "Passionate Mythology," Field wrote:

> In the soft, hazy twilight the members were seated
> In elegant drawing-room high in the sky.
> With nectar ambrosial their bosoms were heated
> And Venus sat smiling on Jupiter's thigh.

Mars went up to Juno and swore upon honor
 He'd make it all right and she'd nothing to fear.
He settled the question by mounting upon her
 And into her thrust the whole length of his spear.

If the women, who were so emphatically denied access to Field's male fellowship, were, nonetheless, provided mythic proportions when entered into poetry—to wit: "Our Lady Lil" and "The Fair Limousin"—this was only better to illustrate the virtues of their male counterparts. As in the case of "Poor Juno," who, upon yielding to Mars, must pay the consequences (". . . he tore the partition / That parted her quiff from her dirty arse-hole"), so also must Lil and the Fair Limousin yield to the superior male The unfortunate Lady Lil who "was the best our [mining] camp produced" had "wore the grass half off the hill; / 'Till finally, she missed her shot, / and Short Pete had her on the pot."

But she died game, just let me tell,
And had her boots on when she fell,
So what the hell, Bill, what the hell!

Or, as in the case of the Fair Limousin, a fate similar to that of Juno is suffered when she must confront Edward and his "brobdingnagian prick":

Her eyeballs rolled up in her head,
 her lips turned black and blue;
But there she lay and sozzled
 'till he pumped her full, and then
He went and hired a doctor
 to sew her up again.

The obvious intention of such sadistically oriented verse was seemingly not so much an attempt to denigrate women as an attempt to attack the false idealism of the age. By going to the extreme opposite of the accepted standards of his time, Field provided a biting antidote to his own popularized verse and the prevailing temper which sought completely to deny the natural and moral significance of physicality. Juno, Lil, and the Fair Limousin (like Julia in "In Imitation of Robert Herrick") are not only the victims of a coarse and sadistic humor, but also they are the victims of a society which forbade any overt sensual pleasures. At the various men's club meetings, such rude humor provided an outlet where the repressed and the tabooed could be vented amidst the congenial atmosphere of coffee and cigars, under circumstances which were not only unthreatening but were shamelessly amusing.

Field's earliest recorded piece of "sub rosa" doggerel, "Slug 14," was read by him at the Printers' Banquet in St. Joseph, Missouri in 1876. Like Denver in the 1880's, St. Joseph was steeped in the accustomed social hypocrisies. The escapades of the inexperienced typesetter in "Slug 14" provided an effective release for the newspapermen who were continually called upon to defend the status quo by means of journalistically embellished language. In "Slug 14," Field described the fatal mistakes of the unfortunate typesetter:

> Why, sir, when there came in a wedding report,
> You ought to have seen that "lead-pounder" cavort!
> He got so confused, and so reckless besides,
> That for "kissing" he set "the groom pissed on the bride!"

Finally, the other newspapermen took it upon themselves to do away with the "wretch" by loading him into a cannon and firing him "on high" till he fell to earth again "completely busted." Field then concludes:

> This is no romance, friends—it's solemn truth,
> Heed it, ye vet'rans, ye ambitious youth,
> Or, if ye doubt, consult with any one
> Who worked with me when this fell deed was done.

In a town such as St. Joseph, it was obvious to Field and his associates that they could not afford to make idle mistakes in their profession and retain their jobs. In fact, although it is doubtful that Field's mistakes were of the same caliber, he would later write Julia from Denver of his contempt for the town's straight-laced morality. "If I were you," urged Field, "I would not stay in St. Joseph any length of time. I hate the town because of reminiscences which scandal inflicted and which will always haunt me like a ghost." Although Field did not mention what the particular scandal was, he obviously held the town and its provincial morality accountable.

By the time Field reached Denver, however, he found in the fast-moving theater crowd which centered about the Tabor Grand Opera House an audience seemingly large-minded enough to appreciate his journalistic talents while holding within its ranks those who could accept his more Rabelaisian nature. As Willard Morse, who was first treasurer and then general manager of the Tabor Grand, recalled, "Field was constantly at the Tabor and met many of his theatrical friends there. I remember particularly Helena Modjeska, Marie Jansen, Emma Abbott, Lawrence Barrett and John McCulloch. Denver," added Morse, "was a regular stopping place for a week's stand of all the large shows on their way to San Francisco. Field wrote, I think, all the theatrical articles that appeared in the *Tribune.*"

Presumably one of Field's first articles was that in which he described the pretentious opening of the Tabor on September 5, 1881, with Emma Abbott in the lead role of "Maritana."

> By half-past 8 o'clock the last carriage had rolled up and deposited its wealth of beauty and chivalry, and the large audience anxiously awaited the rise of the curtain. The display of elegant toilets must have more than satisfied even the most hypercritical and what especially pleased *The Tribune* was the appearance of so large a number of gentlemen in full dress attire.

Though Field doubtlessly enjoyed the pomp and circumstance of the formal opening, there is an irony in his tone which implies his awareness of the thin veneer of respectability which shielded the Tabor Grand from its not-so-distant ancestors. It was, after all, not until the 1850's that Denver had anything approximating formal theater. And even then, these theaters were most often found only adjacent to the bars or gaming tables of Denver's plentiful dance houses. In these so-called theaters—the Platte Valley Theatre, the Palace, and Turner Hall—the "sock and buskin" joined merrily with the gold-digger's boot. And the Tabor Grand, though infinitely more elegant and relatively expensive to attend, diverted many who would have preferred to have been at the remaining dance and vaudeville halls. That Field well understood this conflict of interests is indicated by the paragraph he wrote for the Denver *Tribune*.

> The Dramatic critic is Asleep. The play Does not Interest him. He will give it Thunder in the Paper. The Actors will be sorry when they Read the Paper because it will Say they are not Artists. After the Play, the Critic will go to the Variety Show. Will he Sleep there? No, he will Not. The lady in the Short Dress

and Pink Tights will Buy six Copies of the Paper in the Morning because the Critic will Say she is an Artist. It is very Comfortable to be an Artist when there are Critics in the Neighborhood.

Still, in spite of the risk of suffering such bland fare at the more presentable theaters, those who looked for it could inevitably find sufficient stimulation. Such colorful ladies of the stage as Sarah Bernhardt, Helena Modjeska, and Marie Jansen became famous overnight, as much for their spirited style as for their notable acting ability. While day-to-day life conspired to make women as sexually passive as possible, on the stage they were often portrayed as full-blooded, exotic, and sexually potent. Not surprisingly, clergymen and other crusaders for morality of the late nineteenth century often became the voice pieces for sensational remarks on the character of these glamorized ladies. J. H. McVicker, of McVicker's Theater in Chicago, reported a sermon in 1882 where a reverend of the "Gospel of Charity" declared that "nine out of every ten actresses of to-day are unchaste" and that "ninety-nine out of every hundred opera houses have a saloon, gambling-hall, and a brothel attached."

Whether or not such charges were substantiated, the controversial surroundings of the new actresses permitted Field a latitude in his newspaper verse which he could not find elsewhere. His untempered enthusiasm for Emma Abbott—who tried desperately to effect a relatively sedate image—provoked such unrestrained verses as the following:

> The humble bee that sips and sips
> His fill of honeyed bliss,
> Knows no such joys as Romeo feels

When at fair Abbott's feet he kneels,
Or from her luscious, juicy lips
Inhales an Abbottonian kiss.

What boon could any swain demand
More glorious than this:
To stand among the soft refrains
Of Gounod's most inspiring strains
And clasp a snowy dimpled hand
And breathe an Abbottonian kiss.

On another occasion, Field's popular newspaper verse in "Modjesky as Cameel" tended to bear out the Reverend Herrick Johnson's warning that because of the "demanded excitements" of the actors and actresses "corrupt tastes [were] formed at the theater." In this poem, Helena "Modjesky" is rescued from almost certain corruption by the noble but woolly "Three-Fingered Hoover" who whisks her off stage in the nick of time: " 'Cameel,' sez he, 'your record is ag'in you, I'll allow, / But, bein' you're a woman, you'll git justice anyhow.' "

Similarly, Field deliberately poked fun at the postured respectability of the western audience. In "A Royal Misunderstanding," he wrote:

The prince and the princess with ecstasy viewed
  The role which Miss Anderson played,
And 'twas plain, by the sighs of his highness, the dude,
  That the actress a conquest had made.

"The stage is most fortunate," murmured the prince,
  "Since she brings such a wonderful leg"—

"Oh, hush!" cried his spouse, with a palpable wince—
  "Remember my presence, I beg!"

"My dear, I intended to say," he explained
  "Such a wonderful leg"—"Sir, enough!"
Interrupted the princess, now visibly pained:
  "Have done with this prurient stuff!"

"I didn't mean 'leg,'" cried the prince, "Not a bit!
  "But here's what I meant at the start:
Such a wonderful legacy, as you'll admit,
  Of beauty and genius and art!"

If Denver's untutored "royalty" were known occasionally to misunderstand the theater's interpretation of "beauty and genius and art," the churches (at least in their view) seldom did. As the Rev. Herrick Johnson wrote in his *Plain Talk About the Theater,* "it strips young women of their ordinary attire and exhibits them to the public gaze so that to the eye of the audience they seem, and are meant to seem, almost naked! You do not need to be told," added the reverend, "why that is done."

Field, while obviously not sharing the Reverend Herrick's moral outrage, did share a view—almost a fascination—which tended to regard his theater friends as exempt from society's strictures. The theater's allurement was, in fact, a preoccupation of Field's, dating from the days of his youth. In what would later become characteristic behavior, Field had once threatened his guardian, Melvin Gray, with joining a road show and taking his mentor's name as his stage name. More seriously, he wrote his friend Mrs. John Stockton in 1871 about his intention of becoming a professional actor, noting that he had lately been employed on the St. Louis *Times-Journal* "but am now about to enter upon a life more congenial to my tastes." Although his attempts to fulfill these designs were continually thwarted, he nonetheless kept up his friendships and his affection with people of the stage and, in full measure, they returned both.

These theater companions seemingly afforded multiple benefits for Field. On the one hand, they provided a means for spreading his own reputation. As Francis Wilson so succinctly put it, "we of the stage were absolutely at his command. If he kept us seriously and humorously before the public, we, in turn heralded his poems and stories, acclaimed them, and were delighted to help popularize them and him." Field, for his part, found among his theater companions a way of life which provided an enjoyment he could not find elsewhere.

Actresses such as Madame Modjeska and Marie Jansen were too world-wise to react with horror at his coarser nature. When they were not made the subjects of thinly clothed newspaper bawdry —such as Field's poem about Emma Abbott—these enduring actresses found themselves at the brunt end of his equally teasing personal correspondence. Although never so blatant as that intended for his male friends, Field's letters, which were elaborately drafted in multi-colored inks, pushed the limits of prevailing taste. When Field found himself unable to attend a party given by Marie Jansen—whose fame was based on her singing of the song "Oh Mama"—he expressed his regrets with the following: "If you will send that phonograph down here, I will breathe into its very vitals objugations and epithets so distinctly expressive of my feelings that the machine will never again be competent to Christian service." Or, on another occasion when Field was laid ill with his not infrequent stomach troubles, he ended his letter to Miss Jansen with the wish that "May you never have dyspepsia."

It would compel such merry hell
Your very blood would curdle;
So wanton not with that frail spot
That lies beneath your girdle.

Ever devotedly yours,
Eugene Field

Field's apparent abandonment of inhibitions in this correspondence was no doubt encouraged by the theater's special place in society. J. H. McVicker, in a lecture he delivered at Central Music Hall in Chicago, elaborated on the uniqueness of the theater in relation to the press and pulpit.

> While preachers and editors are set up as models, the world is taught to look upon the actor merely as a rollicking, good-natured, but worthless fellow. When the stage offends, the offense is of the same nature as the exuberance of a spoiled child that oversteps the bounds of decorum in playing with the senior who has humored it. The offense is reprimanded but forgiven, and the play goes on in a more subdued tone.

In his combined roles as a humorist, an aspirant actor, and a practical joker, Field could overstep the bounds of decorum in a way he could not as a newspaper editor. The day before Oscar Wilde was scheduled to speak at the Tabor in the Spring of 1882, Field—in one of his more elaborate pranks—portrayed himself as the renowned aesthete. Dressed in a broad-brimmed felt hat and sporting a flowing rose-colored handkerchief with a white lily clasped in his hand, Field rode through the streets of Denver to the accompanying cheers of the expectant crowd. The stunt ended only as it inevitably had to end when Field—still dressed in his Oscar Wilde outfit—stopped at the Denver *Tribune* for an interview with the managing editor. The response to such antics, however bizarre, seems remarkably tame. Field's friends and readers circulated inflated accounts of the Wilde deception and, in so doing, spread Field's growing reputation still further. So far as Oscar Wilde was concerned (at least according to Charles Dennis), "Field and Wilde met the next day and Wilde took Field's joke in good part, pronouncing it a bit of profitable publicity for his lecture."

Field's career was filled with such pranks—running the gamut from presenting the actress, Minnie Maddern, with a much-heralded gift of chestnut-sized, fake diamonds, to dressing up in a prison suit to greet visitors to his Chicago office. More than serving as a vicarious way for Field to carry out his acting ambitions, these stunts (like his verse in the *Tribune Primer*) served the important function of exposing the thin line separating sham from fashion in American society. And since they were done in a spirit of jest, they—like the transgressions of the stage—might be reprimanded but were almost always forgiven.

Surely, a similar attitude pertained to much of Field's bawdiness—at least amongst his male companions. His dirty jokes and colorful verse served as welcome relief for pent-up sexual urges and provided a safe rebellion against the censors and preachers. As such, even when they were highly personal, they could usually be pardoned. In writing B. B. Cahoon in 1877, Field freely pondered "I am fearful that you may have failed in your hellish designs and again my mind is filled with equally painful suspicions that you may have accomplished them." Then, with unabashed, boyish curiosity, he risked:

Tell this soul with sorrow laden—
Tell me truly, I implore!
Did you screw the Southern Maiden—
Did you f--k the fair Lenore?

Even in his later years, when Field grew less discreet in his personal references, his verses apparently stirred few ill-feelings. Such was the case of his "Bangin' on the Rhine" in which he employed the name of his fellow journalist, Edward Cowen, whom Thompson described as the man who welcomed Field to London in 1889 and remained one of his most intimate friends to the end. That this friendship was not irreparably strained seems truly remarkable in light of such stanzas as the following, which told of "Cowen from Chicago" and his experiences with "good bangin' on the Rhine."

He spread her on the verdant sward beneath the starlight dim
And linked his business end to hers, which she turned up to him.
Upon her lips with garlic moist, his amorous lips were glued
And while his foaming tongue the husky harlot chewed.
Around the hollow of his back he felt her two legs twine,
Ah! that was glorious bangin', good bangin' on the Rhine.

According to the book dealer, Frank Morris, these rhymes along with "A French Crisis" (otherwise known as "Our Fair Limousin") and "Socratic Love" were run off in the press shop of the *Daily News* office on yellow paper in editions of fifty. "They were done at different times," recalled Morris some years later, "and on each occasion when ready he [Field] would start down the street, stop in to see his most intimate friends that understood the humor of it, and hand them a copy."

131

If Field's theater and newspaper friends displayed unusual fortitude in coping with Field's brash humor, so too did his friends of the cloth. The Reverend F. M. Bristol (who, in 1895, gave Field's eulogy address) and the Reverend F. W. Gunsaulus learned to express little surprise when finding their names inscribed on slips of paper attached to books of a Rabelaisian character in Chicago's book shops. The intended recipients of such barbs were, however, as much the conservative parishioners who presumably would be shocked at the alleged purchases of their pastors as the pastors themselves. At the beginning of the century only one in seven Americans belonged to a church; by the end of the century that number had climbed to three in seven, a trend caused not so much by fear of the devil as by fear of community disapproval. As William T. Stead proclaimed in his 1895 study of Chicago, "many of the richer churches in the city are nothing more nor less than social clubs," adding that particularly the Protestant churches had "succumbed largely to the temptation of being at ease in Zion."

In his manner of boisterously striking out at religious complacency, there is a certain similarity in the Field who delighted in yelling across the street for the obvious benefit of his pious neighbors at McCormick Theological Seminary: "No, Charles Henry, I shall never play poker with you again on Sunday night," and the Field who wrote such bawdy lyrics as "The Medieval Maiden's Confession" and the "Mark of the Man-Child." In these poems (discreetly garbed in literary archaisms), Field coupled his attack on the false piety of romantic love with an attack on the similar pieties represented by the church. The "Medieval Maiden" is uncommonly fond of her confessor ("Sweet Clement, this can surely be no sin, / But if it be, pray put it further in"). So, too, the

"Mark of the Man-Child" is found to be more "man" than child. This poem tells the story of a "gentle nun who had never strayed," but who, in painting a picture of the holy babe, seeks the advice of the gardener regarding the child's genitalia or, as quaintly phrased, the "mark of the man-child." After the nun does indeed stray, the Mother Abbess found in the "dim old room / A picture shrouded in dust and gloom."

> One look of horror the Abbess gave,
> Then a laugh rippled over her face like a wave,
> And raising both hands above her head,
> "Mon Dieu! 'tis Patrick's," was all she said.

Field, like Twain, deeply resented that the expression of sexuality seemed to have taken a backward turn since ancient times. And he was particularly sensitive about this when it came to the popular bowdlerized versions of the classics. Field with his brother, Roswell, had taken pains in 1894 to provide his favorite, Horace, with a uniquely modern dress in their freely translated *Echoes from the Sabine Farm.* One verse, however, which was left out of this volume as it appeared in the *Collected Works,* went farther in explaining Field's attitude toward Horace than the actual book itself. In "The Truth About Horace," Field complained "It is very aggravating / To hear the solemn prating / Of the fossils who are stating / That old Horace was a prude." He then concluded in his own inimitable manner:

> He was a very owl, sir,
> And, starting out to prowl, sir,
> You bet he made Rome howl, sir,
>   Until he filled his date;

> With a massic-laden ditty
> And a classic maiden pretty
> He painted up the city,
>   And Maecenas paid the freight!

That Field had neither the moral or literary license of Horace nor a Maecenas to pay the freight was a matter which perplexed Field throughout his career. As he wrote in his "A Lamentation":

> Oh, if I were a poet
> The world would surely know it—
> Ye gods! how I would go it
>   From morning until night!
> I'd write no rhymes jackassic,
> But carmina as classic
> And as redolent of Massic
>   As old Horace used to write!

Still, as much as Field railed at his lack of freedom, there can be little doubt but that so far as "sub rosa" matters were concerned, he believed they should be subject to "elite" scrutiny only. In one of the few serious pieces he wrote on the subject, Field proclaimed, "All books are not for everybody; in literature there is a distinct aristocracy of intelligence. There are many people who should be prevented by law from reading the songs of Solomon. Literature is not so likely to be unfit for readers as readers are likely to be unfit for literature." The obvious implication being that if one were not properly educated he might easily be influenced in immoral ways, or worse, be predisposed to destroy such a valuable heritage.

Field's "Only A Boy," which was considered his sole, earnest attempt at writing erotic prose, provides a soul-rending lesson of

the inherent pitfalls one might expect in the adult sexual world if
he were lacking proper education. The story, which is allegedly
told from the first-person perspective of a gentleman of both age
and experience, details the rapid and premature degeneration inherent in forsaking too early one's books for the pleasures of the
flesh. The narrative begins by explaining that:

> up to my eleventh year, I had known only books and sketching—a
> sweet-tempered linen-dressed boy, who lived out of the sunshine
> and ignored the innocent deviltries of youth; who looked upon
> girls as horrid; whose life was rounded by a pony, books, pictures,
> and the flowers, in the conservatory.

But then, "It came to mine; and on that sweet, singing summer day in my twelfth year, when Cupid threw apart the silken curtains, revealing beauties of which I had not even dreamed, my hand
lost its cunning; to books I said farewell, and ambition was dead."
The provocateur of this nemesis is a thirty-year-old woman visitor
whose husband has been ill for nearly a year, thereby depriving her
of the delights of those who "get married." During the ensuing en-
counters, where the boy proves himself an apt pupil ("I bit her
arms, her belly, her legs; bit and sucked her rosy nipples"), it
soon becomes obvious that he is dealing with a woman of considerable deception. Although she was supposedly "a lady of refinement
and culture," her language belies her appearance. After telling the
boy to "do it to me nice,"—which he does repeatedly—she explains
with the shockingly untutored "Oh! little one, ain't this nice?"
"Nice," perhaps, but after the first encounter, "for the first time
in my life, [I] experienced a high degree of restlessness and impa-
tience. What was it I wanted? I got out my drawings; they had
grown dull and stupid. I turned to my books, but they were un-

satisfying." And finally, upon her departure, "Books, flowers, drawing, pony—all things of the past. The strain at last was too much . . . and on the same bed, so hallowed by lingerings of the past, I was battling with death."

Field's point—however irreverently taken—seems to be that if the boy had not been "only a boy," if only he had restrained himself, studied more, before experiencing the delights reserved for those who "get married," then, surely, the results would not have been so fatal. While Field is obviously spoofing, it is a half-hearted spoof and one which he himself had not worked out in his own consciousness. The narrative concludes in mock-seriousness with the wish for the reader that:

> you will be rewarded with all the pleasurable emotions that you anticipated—that I have written nothing to burst the pantaloons of my gentlemen friends, nor bring the dear girls to the use of a long-necked cologne bottle to quench the flame in their electrical generators, my task is finished.

But many, as might be imagined, could not take such jesting lightly. And Anthony Comstock, as chief agent for the Society for the Suppression of Vice, was one who could not. He embarked on a full-scale campaign for elimination of the story from American society. And notwithstanding a rather substantial circulation, "Only A Boy" was soon hardly to be found outside the libraries of ardent collectors. For Comstock, the idea that the "Laureate of Little Children" had written such a thing was nothing short of heresy. In speaking of much milder texts, he had warned parents to "rid the home of all of Satan's household traps, and whenever you discover one burn it to ashes!" The inherent evils in such stories, he felt, would inevitably "render the imagination unclean, destroy domestic peace, desolate homes, cheapen woman's virtue, and make foul-mouthed bullies, cheats, vagabonds, thieves, desperadoes, and libertines." In short, they would destroy everything in society which Field, in the popular mind, was credited with instilling.

But ultimately if men such as Comstock had little patience for those engaged in the propagation of immoral literature, the men and women closest to Field—who were most responsible for preserving his reputation—never abandoned him. Their loyalty, however, may have survived because they, unlike Comstock, had a greater understanding of the complexities of the man and the age. As Art Young, the cartoonist, would remember, "Field was, perhaps, no more Pagan or Rabelaisian than the rest of us who worked and laughed with him." The only difference being that he, unlike the others, "was always initiating such waggeries and foolishness."

Denver Public Library

Francis Wilson, who, with Field, masqueraded as cherubs, had an abiding sense of loyalty to the men's club bards.

Chicago Historical Society

Field and his fellow devotees of bawdy literature took the greatest precautions when it came to shielding women from possible "contamination." Pictured here: Trotty, Julia, and friends.

In the fast-moving theater crowd which centered about the Tabor Grand, Field found an audience for his Rabelaisian spirit.

Denver Public Library

Denver Public Library

In Denver's dance and vaudeville halls, such as the Palace, the "sock and buskin" joined with the gold-digger's boot.

Chicago Historical Society

J. H. McVicker of McVicker's Theater reported a sermon in 1882 where a reverend declared that "nine out of every ten actresses of today are un-chaste."

New York Public Library

Even actresses such as Emma
Abbott, who tried to create a
relatively sedate image, often
found themselves the subjects of
Field's unrestrained verse.

New York Public Library

Actress Helena Modjeska was one of many who provoked the Reverend Herrick Johnson to take alarm at the "corrupt tastes" of the theater.

New York Public Library

Field's multi-colored correspondence to actress Marie Jansen pushed the limits of prevailing decorum.

Denver Public Library

Field's friends displayed unusual fortitude in coping with his brash and often bawdy humor.

Raymond Mander and Joe Mitchenson Theatre Collection

Field's masquerade as Oscar Wilde resulted in a great deal of publicity for both the British aesthete and the American journalist. Pictured here, Oscar Wilde during his tour of America in 1882.

New York Public Library

Anthony Comstock, as chief agent for the Society for the Suppression of Vice, embarked on a full-scale campaign to have Field's "Only a Boy" eliminated from American circulation.

Chicago:
Politics and Satire

Talk of Field's eccentric personality preceded his arrival in Chicago in 1883. Chicago's *Morning News* editor, Melville Stone, after hearing of Field's extravagant pranks and reading his *Tribune Primer* stories, headed west in the spring of 1883 with the explicit goal in mind of luring Field to the financially greener pastures of Chicago journalism. The terms of his sufficiently tempting offer were that Field should write a column of his own—to "stand or fall by the excellence of his work"—and that he would be paid at a beginning salary of fifty dollars per week.

The Chicago to which Stone introduced Field was one of comparative innocence. As Slason Thompson remembered it, Chicago was "still in the swaddling clothes of civic development." But within the next few years—between 1880 and 1891—her population would increase from 503,298 to 1,099,850; her size would jump from

35.79 square miles to 180.2 square miles; and her wealth would al-most double as it rose from $117,133,726 to $219,354,368.

Field's first regular column—which, within the month, was named "Sharps and Flats" after a popular play of the time—ap-peared on August 16, 1883. The lead stories of the day were char-acteristic of Chicago's optimistic spirit. At Ogden's Grove, ten thousand people had gathered on August 15 to attend the Irish National Demonstration. Amongst them was a reporter for the Chicago *Tribune* whose impassioned account captured well the swirling mixture of patriotism and nationalism which marked the day's tempo. Beneath a cloudless sky "in whose depths an eternal summer seemed to be nestling," the reporter caught sight of "the people of the [Irish] race" who gathered happily with those of other classes. Although they might be "tossed on the crest of en-thusiasm when the fiery and impetuous Finerty stood before them," still they were "social, and orderly, and friendly as they parted in groups and partook of their lunches on the grounds." Little threat was seen even in such an insurrectionary motto as that on the speakers' platform which declared "Burn everything that comes from England except coal" since above this, noted the reporter, "the Red, White, and Blue and the Green hung in the wind side by side." Any potential danger to the picnickers was subdued by the pleasant mood of the waltzing, the talking, and the music. If the English were the common enemy in terms of rhetoric, they were definitely just "good friends," in terms of the warm fellowship of a summer's afternoon.

Besides, Anglo readers could receive further reassurance by glancing over the adjacent front-page account of the British dig-nitaries then visiting the town. While curiosity led the men in the morning to the "great pig-sticking and cattle-slaughtering centre," the "fair Englishwomen, not particularly interested in these bloody scenes, donned their riding habits and rode down to South Park and back." By noon, however, everybody had returned in preparation for the excursion to Pullman where the strangers went into ecstasies over the series of surprises to which they were conducted —the Corliss engine, the shops, the library, the theater, and so forth. The party then adjourned to an elegant dinner at the Hotel Florence where a toast was offered to George Pullman "for his efforts to reconcile capital and labor and make the lot of the workingman happier and better." Ethnic protests, such as that which had occurred earlier in the day at Ogden's Grove, were obviously not a matter for serious concern.

Chicagoans, in the early 1880's, under the leadership of industrialists and intellectuals alike, were rapidly dispelling any lingering doubts about the evils involved in making large sums of money. In a paper read before the Chicago Historical Society on the evening of January 20th, 1880, William Bross advised Chicagoans to do "all that your position and your energy can achieve [because] bless you, friends, the more you prosper, the more you all will contribute to the wealth and the prosperity of Chicago." And similarly, a handbook put out in 1883 chronicling Chicago's growth in fifty years from "a quiet village to a great roaring metropolis where the wheels never cease to whirl and hum," boasted that "all this had been as easy and natural as is that [growth] of the plant when once the seed is sown in good soil." The report continued by stating proudly that all this had been done with "no financial crisis nor labor upheaval" because "the men who engaged in manufacturing in Chicago went about it as they would to build themselves a little home, with no other appeal than the permission to spend their money and develop the resources of the city and its surrounding country."

Businessmen pointed optimistically to the statistics from the "inspectors of manufactories" which indicated that in the three years since the census of 1880 the number of hands "employed in manufacturing" in Chicago had risen from 110,819 to 132,893. Even the announcement of the suspension of Edmund C. Stedman —"the banker-bard of Wall Street"—failed to stem the healthful rise of the stock market on August 16, 1883. On the contrary, "tenders of financial aid aggregating hundreds of thousands of dollars were made to Mr. Stedman during the day, but he felt bound to decline them all, inasmuch as the disaster that had befallen his firm had been brought about by the unwarranted speculations of his son." Such strong humility, in the face of family dishonor, could serve only to bolster the public confidence in the general integrity of the stock exchange and more specifically of the individuals who ran it.

But while Stedman in New York had apparently bridged the gap between finance and literature—if not with complete success, at least with honor—this was a partnership which rested less comfortably in Chicago. Upon his arrival, Field reacted with both shock and fascination at what he termed the "git-up-and-git" culture of the new "Porkopolis"—a city whose highest cultural aspirations seemed predetermined by the whims of her merchants. As Henry B. Fuller, the novelist, put it, Chicago was "the only great city in the world to which all its citizens have come for the avowed purpose of making money. There you have its genesis, its growth, its object; and there are but few of us who are not attending to that object very strictly."

Field, like Fuller, was one of the few who stood far enough apart to be able to attack the prevailing standards. His satirical barbs were often directed against those newly arrived socialites who persisted in measuring the city's cultural attainments with the statistical exactitude of the business community. "It is no wonder," wrote Field in one of his earlier "Sharps and Flats" columns, "that the crème de la crème of our elite lift up their hands, and groan, when they discover that it takes as long to play a classic symphony as it does to slaughter a carload of Missouri razor-backs, or an invoice of prairie-racers from Kansas."

Field then tendered a possible solution to these frustrations— instant, condensed culture. "We have condensed milk, condensed meats, condensed wines," proclaimed Field, "condensed everything but music." Or, on another occasion, he facetiously reported that "the enterprising firm of Plankington, Armour & Co. announces that it is prepared to meet the demands of our literary public by putting into the spring market an entirely new line of canned goods, scheduled and classified, in the prominent trade-catalogues, as 'Condensed Literature.'" These ingenious preparations—epic poetry, ancient history, lyric poetry—suggested Field, would speedily allay the desires of anyone if he would merely "purchase and consume one of these compounds" at the bargain price of twenty-five cents per can.

That Chicago's cultural center of gravity resided at her Union Stock Yards was a fact of life which Field could never fully accept. His dismay was portrayed in his account of "Mr. Heron-Allen, the handsome and talented young hand-reader, [who was] making a barrel of money in Chicago" by delighting the local society leaders with the "flattering pictures he found in their dainty hands." The "pork-line" in a Chicago hand was reported to be "distinct and long" and directly related to the intellectual or literary line which invariably caused "the wearer to take pleasure in literature, to join literary clubs, to inquire into the mysteries of summer philosophy, to subscribe to local trade weeklies, to buy handsome wallpaper, and to have the seaside novels rebound in half-calf." Field then added that if it were not for the common occurrence of this latter line "the newsboys would sell mighty few books on our trains, and Billy Pinkerton would never have become famous as an actor."

Nor was it so serious to Field's way of thinking that the pork-line and the literary line rested in such easy proximity, as that the quantitative measurements of the former were so indiscriminately used in judging the qualitative worth of the latter. When George Pullman donated 5,100 books to start a library in his company town, the annual fiscal report boasted that "most" of the library's collection was on "serious subjects" while "only 31 per cent of the books [were] classed as fiction and juvenile." Or similarly, a report on the book trade for 1883 noted that a "gratifying feature" had been "the large increase in the demand for the highest grade of standard works, while the more trashy kinds of cheap publications [had shown] a declining sale." For those accustomed to judging success by volume and dollar, the important part was how *much* was provided. In art as in industry, it was the production quota which invariably received the first attention.

Field's attacks against Chicago's "porkpackers" were dictated less by a strong political conscience than by a revulsion against cultural shams and pretensions. Although the tactics he employed in desanctifying Chicago's "sacred cows" at times resembled those of the emergent reformers, his loyalties were unabashedly Republican.

At the time of the national elections in 1884, Field remained a supporter of James G. Blaine despite strong opposition from his colleagues on the *Morning News* who generally favored Cleveland. On election day, 1884, Field's "Sharps and Flats" column contained a "symposium" of verse designed to undercut the politics of the opposition parties. Beneath a heading of "Rhymes for All Readers" he portrayed the Prohibitionists as rallying the "voters, to the polls" to let their "ballots drop."

> For that which fortifies our souls—
> The genial ginger pop!

While the suffragists were heard to plea, "Stand to your rolling-pins, oh, men, / In patriotic manner— / A tireless zeal should fire you when / A petticoat's your banner!"

As far as the Democrats and the Mugwumps were concerned, Field dismissed them both with a sardonic flourish of his pen. They were depicted as too far afield in their subversion of patriotic principles:

> The mugwump and the democrat
>   With honest fervor mix,
> To kill the crime which shame begat,
>   The Fraud of Seventy-six!

Yet, when all was said and done, and the Democrats did, indeed, win the election, Field's attitude lacked signs of genuine dismay. As Slason Thompson recalled:

> On the day it was finally conceded that Cleveland had carried New York, Field enveloped himself in a shroud of newspapers,

laid himself out across the city department floor, and summoned all the Democrats, Mugwumps, Greenbackers and Equal Rights Suffragists in the office to tramp across his prostrate but unregenerate Republican form. The invitation was accepted with amiable hilarity.

Field's politics, like his satire, were essentially those of debunkery. Thompson remembered that Field rarely, if ever, took the trouble to vote, and that, in fact, Field had no "serious views on political questions. He left the salvation of the republic and the amelioration of the general condition of mankind, to those who felt themselves 'sealed' to such missions." Yet, if his Republicanism was ever called into question, Field was known to react with unexpected fervor.

In response to one such challenge from his Aunt Julia in 1888, Field replied: "I'd like to know what has induced you to suspect that I am or that I ever could be anything but a Republican." He then added reassuringly, "Don't you worry a bit about this branch of the Field family; we still travel under the flag and right up next to the band wagon."

Perhaps what had prompted Aunt Julia's query and Field's own patriotic response was the charged mood of the times. During the few short years since Field's arrival in Chicago, the atmosphere which characterized the Irish Day Picnic—a climate which had encouraged the intermixing of social and economic classes—had virtually disappeared. Chicago's parks—previously the settings of good fellowship and music—now displayed the battle scars of violent confrontations between labor and management. In the face of such incomprehensible acts, Field further retreated to the party of his youth which stood for law, order, and national unity.

By May 1, 1886, Chicago's headlines blazed with the tales of out-and-out rebellion: "Three Thousand Milwaukee Brewers Strike Today," "Five Hundred Men Out at Indianapolis," and even more frightening, "The Crisis at Hand—Railroad Freight Handlers on Two Lines Have Gone Out." At the time of Field's arrival, Chicagoans had pointed with pride to the rapid rise in employment and the seemingly indomitable health of the stock exchange; but by May 1, 1886 a front-page headline reported: "The Trade Situation—Naturally It Is Unfavorably Affected by the Labor Troubles." The accompanying story complained: "There are at least 50,000 employees on strike, against 43,000 last week. The New York Stock Market was inactive during the first part of the week, but has been depressed and feverish in the last three days."

Then, on May 4, 1886 an incident occurred which was so violent and of such proportions that there was space for no other news—save this—on the front pages of Chicago's papers. At Haymarket Square, between Desplaines and Halsted streets, some 1,500 demonstrators had gathered on behalf of several men who had been killed earlier by police during a disruption at the McCormick harvester works. At first, the gathering had seemed surprisingly tranquil. Chicago's Mayor Harrison and the chief of police attended the rally, but then went home when there appeared to be no danger of serious disruption. In leaving, they gave Police Inspector Bonfield the duty of "keeping the peace." A short while later, Bonfield, upon hearing that violence was being advocated by one of the speakers, sent in his troops to break up the meeting. As one press account put it, "the glittering stars were no sooner seen than a large bomb was thrown into the midst of the police [and] spectators." Rioting erupted instantaneously. When it subsided, amidst the rubble were found the bodies of seven police officers and numerous bystanders, whose precise number and identity could never be determined.

Whether or not the actual bombing had been an anarchist plot was a matter for considerable speculation. Regardless, in the minds of most Americans the line between law and open rebellion had been stretched to a precarious state. Cries were heard that something had to be done. And, ultimately, when forced to make a choice between what seemed to be the only two possible alternatives—law or anarchy—most did not hesitate to pick the law. A jury trial, presided over by Judge Gary with the moral backing of the nation's press, convicted eight of the alleged anarchist leaders for inciting violence, and saw to it that four of them were hanged. As Graham Taylor, the founder of the Chicago Commons Social Settlement, later admitted, "I shared the country-wide endorsement of their conviction and penalty." Taylor, a noted social reformer, clearly stood with the majority who felt that the law must be upheld.

On the morning of November 14, 1887, a funeral march—comprised almost entirely of foreigners—filled the streets of Chicago. But in spite of their numbers, which were nearly 5,000, the grave demeanor and somber sympathetic mood stamped indelibly the marching crowd as a funeral procession and not an exhibition of defiance. As such it was recognized and, noted the account in the Chicago *Tribune,* "as such it was protected by the very law that a few short hours before had put to death the men it mourned."

The single disruption in the march was one which ironically stood more for the restoration of the peace than anything else. The *Tribune* reporter noted that "As the procession reached the viaduct a sensational incident occurred. A new head arrived, a man bearing a small American flag inscribed with the battles through which it had been carried twenty-five years ago." The man was Private H. G. Trogden, "known to fame" as the only man to survive the unsuccessful assault on Vicksburg of May 22, 1863. He reached the outside of the Rebel fortifications, planted his banner, and remained under cover until darkness when he was able to return to the Federal lines. Trogden's daring had obviously not diminished during the passing of the years. The newspaper account continued that he "sprang into the line of march unexpectedly and unasked." And when asked to leave, "he waved his flag and kept on his way undaunted by scowls and muttered curses."

Field saw Trogden not as a defiant protester but as a loyal American. And in a poem he wrote for the *Morning News,* Field proclaimed:

> Over the bloody carmine pall,
> Over the vengeful hearts and all
>
> Floated the flag, and none so bold
> To wrench that flag from the old man's hold!
>
> Teach us, old man, that we may know
> The patriot valour of long ago;
>
> Teach us that we may feel no fear
> When viprous enemies appear;
>
> And teach us how sweet 'twould be to die
> Under the flag you raised so high!

Field's ire seemed partially prompted by his personal admiration for the courageous act of Private Trogden and partially it seemed the result of that matter of which he wrote his Aunt Julia, that he himself wished to be counted amongst those closest to the bandwagon and under the flag. Although the final verses, as they appeared in the *Morning News,* bore the initials "S.T.F.," this was due not so much to Field's humility, as his acknowledgment of the unasked-for assistance of Melville Stone and Slason Thompson. Both had disagreed with Trogden's protest—and, according to Charles Dennis, edited Field's verses "so barbarously that Field declined to acknowledge them as his literary offspring." Dennis then added that "I thought then and I think now that the changes made in it against Field's protests were useless or worse."

Such censorship was not uncommon to Field. Early in his career he devised the tactic of inserting two or three particularly offensive paragraphs in his column for no other reason than to have them blue-penciled out. In this way, his other, often equally abrasive writings might slip by unnoticed. But obviously this practice was as much a game for Field as a serious proposition. His fellow journalist James C. Young once wrote that "whenever one of these items passed the censor it was a day of glee for Field . . . [it] gave him all the thrill of a boy who had fooled his teacher."

Because of Field's perpetual challenges to his editor-teachers he seemed to require constant supervision. Even Dennis, who was understandably critical of the censorship by Thompson and Stone, admitted that in his duties as managing editor for the *Morning News* (after 1891) he occasionally found himself "compelled by [his] sense of duty to butcher Field's copy unmercifully." And although the yoke of censorship was apparently lifted somewhat after Victor Lawson bought out Stone's share of the *Daily News* in 1888, Field was never as free in editorial discretion as popular opinion would have it. Field's Chicago editors desired all the caustic flavor of his Denver writings without the attendant libel suits.

Even the relatively open-minded Lawson sent Field the following Christmas Eve (1894) memo. As Lawson so succinctly put it, the "Sharps and Flats" column "in Saturday's paper suggests the following pointers":

> George B. Swift—Do not belittle or criticise his mayorality candidacy.
> A. C. Durborrow—Do not boom his mayorality candidacy.
> Major Harry F. Donovan—You are prone to be altogether too kind to Mr. Donovan. He is distinctly "no good."
> Carse vs Hobbs—Hobbs is all right, and Carse is all wrong. This on general principles, with a distinct application in the present distribution of midway proceeds.
>
> Very truly yours,
> Victor F. Lawson

As the most widely quoted paragrapher in the nation, it was inevitable that restraints on Field would not necessarily always be either as direct or as negative as those of Lawson. After Field wrote favorably of Hooley's Theater in Chicago, Harry J. Powers, the manager, penned a quick note of appreciation: "Your paragraph in Saturday's *Record* has just been shown to me. Thank you very much 'Gene' and may God bless you and yours." Or similarly, John R. Tanner from the Third District of the Republican State Central Committee wrote Field just before election day, 1894: "I hardly know how to thank you for your valuable utterings in 'Sharps and Flats,' in the *Record*. Allow me to say that I feel *very* grateful and will call in person when the battle is over."

Ultimately, then, it was personalities rather than politics which appeared to hold the greatest sway over Field's own editorial decisions. During the summer of 1894, Chicago once again experienced the pain of labor and management upheaval. In what was no doubt a bleak omen of the coming events, the Chicago *Tribune* on May 1, 1894, published a front-page cartoon, forthrightly entitled: "Ready to Release the Pack." The cartoon depicted a shirt-sleeved man on his knees under the banner of "American Labor," while above him stood a well-dressed man holding three angry dogs, aptly named: "Free Trade," "Foreign Competition," and "Cheap Labor." That the shirt-sleeved man would not turn and run, but would make a most violent attack on the dog's owner was something which even the most astute of *Tribune* readers would probably not have guessed. And what would have surprised them even more, if they were accustomed to reading Field's "Sharps and Flats" column in the Chicago *Record,* was that Eugene Field— the man who was traditionally "under the flag"—would side with the man on bended knee.

Just a little over a week after the cartoon made its appearance —on May 11, 1894—the Pullman workers, who represented America's ideal city, went on strike. At first, little was changed. The weather remained warm, sunny and pleasant. And visitors to Pullman's Arcade Park found family groups lounging and picnicking on the grass. Yet, in the midst of all this, Pullman discreetly departed to the seclusion of his private island in the St. Lawrence River. When he returned more than a month later, he found his Arcadian community almost beyond salvation.

During Pullman's absence, it became obvious to those living in Chicago that his town was not quite the ideal it had been touted. As the Reverend William Carwardine discovered: "To the casual visitor [it] is a veritable paradise; but it is a hollow mockery, a sham, an institution girdled with red tape." By April of 1894, nearly one-fourth of the shop employees had been making thirty-one dollars or less while average monthly rental for the model homes remained at fourteen dollars. Inquisitive reporters soon discovered a previously ignored section of the town where instead of the customary "bungalows," they found unpaved and unsewered streets lined with three-room "hovels" lacking indoor plumbing.

As Chicago newspapers—led by the Chicago *Times*—increasingly focused their attacks on the figure of George Pullman, Field, rather inadvertently, found himself at the forefront of the movement. It became customary for Chicago papers to refer to Pullman as the "Baron" or "Duke," while drawing comparisons between his town and a feudal manor. One such article in the previously supportive Chicago *Inter Ocean* commented on the "feudal-like" behavior of management's refusal to negotiate with the workers.

> Apparently to reach the high administrative ideal aimed at the management of this "model industrial tenement" by the Marquis de Pullman . . . there is nothing needed but the knout, a liberal supply of shackles, and cheap transport to Siberia.

What the reporter for the Chicago *Inter Ocean* was saying, in fact, was what Field had been saying in his debunking attacks on Chicago's sham culture for a long time. Some years earlier when George Pullman had received an honorary title of nobility from King Humbert I of Italy, Field had suggested in "Sharps and Flats" that Pullman might feel most comfortable with the title of *marchese* or, as Field indicated it might be pronounced in Chicago, "markeesy." Admittedly, added Field, Pullman would prefer to be called a chevalier, "but we are inclined to think that markeesy sounds just a trifle more bong tong than sheevalya, and we hope that Mr. Pullman will choose that title." Field then mockingly

163

deplored "the existence of a bitter malice against the Markeesy di Pullman in certain local society circles" which had been responsible for the following "ribald song":

When the party is breezy and wheezy
And palpably greasy, it's easy
    To coax or to wring,
    From a weak-minded king,
The titular prize of markeesy.

By July of 1894 Field, along with many others, began to look more seriously at the inherent flaws in the kingdom of the Markeesy di Pullman. As Jane Addams later recalled, "Those of us who lived in Chicago during the summer of 1894 were confronted by a drama which dispelled the good nature which in happier times envelops the ugliness of the industrial situation."

The chief figures in this drama, as in the cartoon, were George Pullman as the markeesy versus the members of the American Railway Union under the leadership of Eugene V. Debs. Field had first met Debs the preceding year when Field had presented him with several autographed copies of his poetry and prose. But it was not until July of 1894 that this previously casual relationship was put to its most severe and ultimately enduring test. Just as Field had once singled out Private Trogden as the little guy caught in the aftermath of the Haymarket violence, Field now apparently overcame his political preferences to come to the aid of his friend Debs.

On July 2, with an estimated 50,000 men away from their railway jobs and supporting a city-wide boycott, U.S. Attorney General Richard Olney, with President Cleveland's sanction, succeeded in gaining a court injunction against all attempts to impede the movements of trains or mail. The next day, large groups of strikers, ignoring the injunction, gathered at the Rock Island yard in Blue Island. On July 4, under Olney's orders, U.S. troops from Fort Sheridan were rushed to Chicago. As they paraded by the gracious homes on the northern fringe of the city, Field's suburban neighbors ran to the marching ranks and offered flowers. But when the soldiers reached the working-class neighborhoods, sullen crowds taunted them.

With the arrival of the troops, the strikers escalated their destruction of the railroad property at the Union Stock Yards. And although Debs, time and again, promised an end to the boycott if Pullman would only arbitrate with the strikers, Pullman adamantly refused all such gestures. By this time, the tide of public opinion—confronted with the seeming dichotomy between law and anarchy—swung once again toward the law. Readers of the Chicago *Tribune* were warned in a front-page headline: GUNS AWE THEM NOT—DRUNKEN STOCKYARDS RIOTERS DEFY UNCLE SAM'S TROOPS— MOBS INVITE DEATH.

In the midst of this chaos, Eugene Field found time, on July 7, to jot off a personal note: "Dear Debs: You may require the services of a loyal friend by and by. When that time comes, let me know." And on the following day, Field described his divided loyalties to the readers of his "Sharps and Flats" column.

> Mr. Debs is, to our thinking, laboring in serious error just at present, but we do not question his sincerity, because we know him personally, and we know him to be a sincere, earnest, honest man. George M. Pullman may be right and E. V. Debs may be wrong; let us presume so. And having granted that much, this

much can be added with positiveness: if ye be ill, or poor, or starving, or oppressed, or in grief, your chances for sympathy and succor from E. V. Debs are 100 where your chances with G. M. Pullman would be the little end of nil whittled down.

As Debs persistently refused to call off his boycott, increasing demands were heard to "get Debs" for contempt of court. His unyielding stance was met with accusations that questioned his sanity. The New York *Times* went so far, on July 9, as to report that Debs was not only a drunkard but that he was the victim of a "disordered condition of mind and body." Confronting such attacks, Field warned his "Sharps and Flats" readers on July 11 that "in case Debs is apprehended and tried upon the charges which are made against him, we presume no difficulty will be had in proving his insanity by these very same newspaper experts who are proclaiming him a mental wreck." He then further advised his readers on July 12 that "in our wrath we may forget that E. V. Debs is, like the rest of us, human. So let us speak of him rather in pity than in anger."

Finally, on July 17, after the boycott had been broken by sheer force and the federal troops had cleared Chicago's tracks, Debs was indicted on contempt charges. And Field, in a last effort to clear the character of his friend—who later served a six-month sentence—told his readers on July 16 that "the newspaper portraits of E. V. Debs are not accurate. Five minutes with him would suffice, we think, to convince a reader of human nature that Debs is a man of high ideals, honest convictions, unswerving integrity, great intellectual vigor (or, perhaps, rather zeal), exceptional simplicity of character and consummate impracticality. His traits," added Field regretfully, "are those, we believe, which, bunched, are very likely to get him into trouble."

After Debs was released from prison in 1895, Field made plans to visit him at Woodstock, New York. "You are settled in your summer quarters," wrote Field, "and I'll soon be out to see you." But, as Debs would sadly recall, "A day or two later I picked up the morning paper to note with profoundest sorrow the announcement of his death."

For Field, as for Jane Addams, the events of 1894 "dispelled the good nature" of happier times. But in their stead and for wont of a certain lost levity, Field, for the first time, had been able to infuse his columns with some of the same "unswerving integrity" which he had so venerated in Debs. For at least one unforgettable moment, Field had been no longer merely the schoolboy playing foolish pranks on his teacher. He had seen the seriousness of society's judgment and instead of mocking its foolishness—as was his usual practice—he bravely, if briefly, tried to halt the injustice. Debs remembered that Field's loyalty came "at a time when intense bitterness prevailed, and when such an avowal meant ostracism and execration." Yet Field's ability to pay the price with no thought of later reward was as much a tribute to his convictions at it was, in fact, a compliment to the stature of his reputation.

Chicago Historical Society

During Field's years in Chicago, from 1883 to 1895, the city would grow tremendously, with her population passing the million mark. Pictured here, commerce at Rush Street Bridge and the Chicago River.

Chicago Historical Society

The Union Stock Yards provided a major tourist attraction for visitors to Chicago in the late-nineteeth century.

Chicago Historical Society

In his "Sharps and Flats" column, Field deftly lampooned the residents of the stately mansions of the "Porkopolis." Lake Shore Drive, *c.* 1893.

Chicago Historical Society

In the aftermath of the Haymarket Square Riot, Field wished to be counted among those closest to the bandwagon and under the flag. Haymarket Square, *c.* 1892.

Chicago Historical Society

When Field got one of his more offensive paragraphs past his censors at the *Daily News*, it gave him all the thrill of a boy who had fooled his teacher. Newsprint arriving at *Daily News* office.

Chicago Historical Society

For several years preceding the Pullman Strike of 1894, Field had been lambasting the foibles of Chicago's "Markeesy di Pullman." George M. Pullman (seated) and family at Castle Rest.

Chicago Historical Society

U.S. troops encamped on the spacious lawns of the Hotel Florence during the strike of 1894.

Chicago Historical Society

Referring to the strike, Jane Addams recalled the drama which dispelled the good nature of the industrial situation. Pictured here, soldiers clowning at the Pullman Works, 1894.

New York Public Library

Eugene V. Debs received Field's strong support. Field asked his readers to speak of Debs "rather in pity than in anger."

Chicago: Sentiment and Success

Shortly before Field's death, in 1895, a brief poem by the Reverend J. P. Hutchinson appeared in the columns of the Chicago *Record*. It was entitled simply: "To Eugene Field."

> I have not looked upon your face,
>   Have never grasped your hand,
> But in your writings I can trace
>   A soul I understand.
>
> Your strains so tender and so true
>   A genial warmth impart,
> Because your pen is dipped into
>   The inkstand of the heart.

The sentiments expressed by the Reverend Hutchinson captured well the feelings of many who, though their feelings might go unrecorded, nonetheless felt an almost overwhelming attachment to the man who had, indeed, so artfully dipped his pen into "the inkstand of the heart." By the early 1890's, Field's writings in "Sharps and Flats" had come to represent Chicago's very pulse and heartbeat—the poet-journalist's depiction of the compendious relief map that was, in actual fact, the daily news.

During the 1890's, with a circulation of more than 160,000, the Chicago *Daily News* grew to be far more influential than either the *Inter Ocean,* the Chicago *Times,* or the *Tribune.* Winning—before the century was over—three times as many readers as the *Tribune,* the *News* achieved a fame of its own as the paper that could be believed.

Surely much of this reputation had been developed through the confidence which Eugene Field had instilled in his fans and readers. If Field was known to be humorous, almost sacrilegious, in dealing with the foibles of Chicago's plutocrats, there were, nonetheless, few who doubted his sincerity in dealing with matters of the heart. With increasing frequency Field's columns grew to encompass those softer qualities of the human temperament. Amidst the confusion of the day, the hour, and the minute—transposed on the pages of the *Daily News*—Field's column provided a certain welcome relief from city tensions. As Reverend Bristol had so eloquently put it in Field's funeral oration, his writing had come to embody "the greatness of faith, hope and love; the greatness of the child spirit."

Even in dealing with the theater or politics, Field increasingly provided his readers with a humorous but tasteful fare, guaranteed to set well with their morning eggs and cereal. By 1893, Field could tell Hamlin Garland in an interview that before he could write about daily activities they "have to get pretty misty."

The confidence which Field generated amongst his readers was made manifest not only by poems such as that by the Reverend Hutchinson, but even more often by those who came to him seeking advice and support. Edgar Lee Masters in his *Tale of Chicago* told of the tens of thousands of youths who came to Chicago in the early Nineties, seeking to breathe the larger air of the city's theaters and amusements. Before arriving they would have read "Sharps and Flats" and marvelled at Field's familiarity as he wrote of Bernhardt, of Joe Jefferson, of the literary figures of New York. He himself had lived in Missouri and had gone to school at a freshwater college in Illinois; and now he belonged to this great world of the city. Surely it was not uncommon for Field to receive letters such as that sent by Jean Blewett of Blenheim, Ontario. "Will you aid me in procuring a situation on a paper," wrote the aspiring young reporter. "I give you the word of a true-hearted Canadian girl that I will trouble you as little as pos-sible—*while ever remembering.* Living so much of my life in this quaint town I am necessarily ignorant of many things, but I can learn and *will* learn."

Others, who would rise to even greater fame and perhaps go off in directions of their own, looked upon Field with a similar veneration and respect. Theodore Dreiser remembered that "dur-ing the year 1890 I had been formulating my first dim notion as to what it was I wanted to do in life. For two years and more I had been reading Eugene Field's 'Sharps and Flats,' and through this I was beginning to suspect, vaguely at first, that I wanted to write, possibly something like that."

Charles Dennis, his own position clearly secure, wrote in 1891 with untempered admiration for Field's meteoric rise and ability.

Tall, slender, boyish, blonde and aggressive, this promising young man came out of the West eight years ago. During those years the growth of his powers has been continuous and rapid. Lighthearted and kindly, fond of friends and yet a scholarly man, devoted to his family, and a little child among children, he has been learning [the] lessons of his art in a variety of schools.

The feats of this "little child among children" were even more remarkable in Dennis's view when it came to Field's ability to produce beautiful poetry and prose virtually on demand.

A poem or a story grows in his mind for days and sometimes for weeks or months before a word of it is written. Finally its turn comes, and then the whole is set down in all haste. Apparently, there is never a lack of subjects. The trouble lies mainly in the picking and choosing.

Field's obvious ease in picking and choosing had been dramatically illustrated when, in 1888, he had written "Little Boy Blue" —the poem whose reputation would so escalate in the coming years that eventually the poet and the poet's creation would become synonymous in the minds of thousands. Field himself had reported that "My 'Little Boy Blue' was written within the space of two hours in the *Record* office to fill an order from the *America*."

And his biographer, Slason Thompson, seemingly endorsed this description in concept if not in actual detail. By this time Thompson had retired from the *Daily News* to found the short-lived, weekly journal called *America*. In this, his initial issue, dated April 7, 1888, Thompson sought literature which would lend a certain distinction to his early efforts. But, in spite of his claims of authorship for the first four words in the last lines—*"What has become of* our Little Boy Blue / Since he kissed them and put them there"—he steadfastly denied having suggested the actual topic.

In fact, noted Thompson, "the truth is, 'Little Boy Blue' was written without any special suggestion or personal experience attending its conception and composition. It was an honest child, begotten of the freest and best genius of Field's fancy."

Dennis obviously went along with Thompson's comments regarding the powers of Field's fancy, but seemed to refute Field in one minor detail by saying that actually Field had *not* written the poem at the *Record* office but rather "he wrote it in bed one April night and read it to me as soon as he reached the office [the] next morning." Dennis then added that "he recognized at once that it was a remarkable production. I was enthusiastic about it, and his smiling satisfaction with the lines told plainly that he saw no way to improve them."

In any case, it soon became apparent to all that "Little Boy Blue"—despite the haste of its execution—captivated the heartstrings of the nation. The record of its popular acclaim which, in turn, escalated the reputation of Eugene Field, is duly recorded. The same issue of *America* which contained "Little Boy Blue" had also a poem by James Russell Lowell entitled "St. Michael the Weigher." Lowell's poem told the story of the poet witnessing St. Michael's weighing of the "hope of Man" against the divine universe:

> Seeing then the beam divine
> Swiftly on this hand decline,
> While Earth's splendor and renown
> Mounted light as thistle-down.

The two poems, though both dealing with the omnipotence of divine power in man's universe, were as opposite in temperament as was conceivable. Yet the competition between the two in the popular marketplace fascinated Field and his newspaper colleagues. As Charles Dennis later remembered it:

> There speedily developed a curious race for popularity between Lowell's poem and "Little Boy Blue," a race that was watched with very great interest by Field and myself. Here was the product of a poet of long-established reputation pitted against that of a mere aspirant to the title of poet. Which would receive the greatest degree of recognition from the newspapers of the country? We kept a close lookout, searching daily the columns of the hundreds of newspapers that came to the office. Both poems were widely copied. Wherever found, we clipped them and matched the two sets of clippings numerically against each other. To Field's immense satisfaction "Little Boy Blue" soon began to outrun its more pretentious rival. Its lead grew longer day by day, until there was no doubt that the younger poet's verses had scored a notable success over Lowell's in point of newspaper popularity.

Whether or not Lowell was aware of it, Field in pitting the talents of his own "Little Boy" against those of "Mike"—as he endearingly referred to the two—was merely adding further kindling to a continuing battle. Field, for some time, had been baiting Lowell in his "Sharps and Flats," apparently beginning when Lowell had refused an invitation to speak in Chicago. In Field's words, "Col. Lowell appears to have regarded it much as he would the cheap effort of a country debating-club, or a commonplace literary lyceum." But then, when Lowell changed his mind, he merely added insult to refusal by reading a critical address on the authorship of *Richard III* delivered previously at Edinburgh instead of his scheduled talk on American politics. Field, in marked anger, wrote, "We regard it as the severest joke ever played upon our community." And then, in a line which surely spoke tellingly of future circumstances, he remarked on the comments of a "well-known art-connoisseur and dealer in leaf-lard" who proclaimed, "This man Lowell is a scholar and a nice gentleman—there's no denying *that:* but, do you know, after all, I think I prefer Bill Nye."

But even Field, who was by this time acquiring a keen appreciation of consumer preferences of the book mart, would have had difficulty in foreseeing the ironic similarity between his chiding of the man who allegedly placed an order for Lowell's books provided the whole set cost more than a hundred dollars and the later auctioning of the manuscript of his own "Little Boy Blue" for an incredible $2,400 at an Allied War Bazaar in 1917.

The story of the success of "Little Boy Blue" was, in large degree, the story of Field's own success. As Charles Dennis wrote, it was this poem which touched off "the widespread affection for Field and his verses. It was speedily set to music. It was read in the schools." Dennis even reported hearing of a friend who had visited the far-off Shetland Islands, and found there the school children—"whose only toys were sea shells and who sucked dried fish for sweeties"—reciting "Little Boy Blue."

"Little Boy Blue" was by no means the first of Field's sentimental verse, and it was even more decidedly not the last. Shortly after the appearance and favorable reception of "Little Boy Blue," there flourished from the pen of Eugene Field such a stock of verse that his friends and colleagues found it was all they could do to keep pace with the output. Charles Dennis fondly recalled the fervor which Field exhibited in the wake of "Little Boy Blue." "At first he was eager to produce many pieces of 'Alaskan balladry.' Later he hit upon the idea of writing lullabies for children of all lands. He was also making notes at this time of his Western mountain experiences for a series of poems dealing with life in a Colorado mining camp. Then came to him the plan of writing paraphrases of Horace."

At this time, the frenzy of activity—the continual probing and testing of subject and style—consumed Field's every moment. Dennis recalled how Field remained propped up in bed, long after midnight, scribbling out his verses. Then, with the coming of the next day, he would rush to the office to consult with Dennis concerning his progress. These midnight products, according to Dennis, "naturally were weighed by him with some anxiety when they confronted him in the cold light of day." But even then, added Dennis modestly, "I am not so conceited as to think that I exercised more than the remotest influence in the final shaping of the poems of that period."

Virtually all these poems eventually wound up in "Sharps and Flats" where Field's readers marveled at them as much for their beauty as their sheer volume. On some days his column was filled to the margins with nothing but poetry. During the first few months of 1889 there was scarcely a day which passed without some new product being issued. The first poem of this series, which eventually became one of his most popular, appeared on New Year's Day 1889 under the title "Casey's Table D'Hôte" ("Oh, them times on Red Hoss Mountain in the Rockies fur away,— / There's no sich place nor times like them as I kin find to-day!"). In his search for alluring subject matter, Field's memory recaptured romantic visions of the occasional trips he had made to the older mining camps of Colorado during his years on the Denver *Tribune.* That Field had hardly found time or impetus to venture from his city desk while in Denver made little difference to the readers of the *Daily News*. What was more important—amidst the din of railway engines and stockyards—was that there was at least someone who was willing to pretend. Similar flights of Field's imagination carried him back to a time when people seemed less concerned with formalities of calling cards as in his "Good-by and God Bless You" ("This seems to me a sacred phrase, / A thing come down from righteous days."). Or, as was far more often the case, he would decide to paraphrase his friend Horace of the distant Elysian fields—such as "When you were mine in Auld Lang Syne" (from Horace III.9). Certainly most popular with his newspaper fans were Field's trips to the nursery. And so, in March 1889, the readers of "Sharps and Flats" were treated to an artful assemblage of transposed lullabies—the "Cornish Lullaby," the "Orkney Lullaby," the "Norse Lullaby," and even the "Japanese Lullaby." And then, on March 11, for the first time ever, "Wynken, Blynken and Nod"—in that most successful of journeys—"sailed off in a wooden shoe." Of the writing of this particular poem, Field later recalled: "The little story occurred to me as I was riding home on the street cars." He then explained that although he first intended to focus on a "windmill story," when the names of "Wynken, Blynken and Nod" occurred to him he "took up with the wooden shoe."

> I sat up in bed and wrote out the lullaby as it now appears, with the exception that I first wrote "Into a sea of blue," and this line I changed next morning to "Into a sea of dew." The original draft of these verses was made upon brown wrapping paper.

But if Field's lullabies seemingly indicated an uncanny capacity for production, they were soon to be outdone by his spectacular performance in early April. On April 4, 1889, in an early celebration of the first-year anniversary of "Little Boy Blue," Field expanded his usual column to a column and a half and filled it with nine separate poems. Eight of these poems were written in the form of translations or adaptations of either Horace or other poets, even a Heine "Love Song":

> Many a beauteous flower doth spring
>   From the tears that flood my eyes,
> And the nightingale doth sing
>   In the burthen of my sighs.
>
> If, O child, thou lovest me,
>   Take these flowerets fair and frail,
> And my soul shall waft to thee
>   Love songs of the nightingale.

Still, it was not the translations and adaptations which lasted longest in the popular imagination, but rather the ninth poem which was written in dialect verse. In "Our Two Opinions," Field told the story of two young men who grew up hating each other and then went off to fight in the Civil War:

> Jim never come back from the war again,
>   But I hain't forgot that last, last night
> When, waitin' f'r orders, us two men
>   Made up 'nd shuck hands, afore the fight.
> 'Nd, after it all, it's soothin' to know
>   That here I be 'nd yonder's Jim,—
> He havin *his* opinyin uv *me*,
>   'Nd I havin' *my* opinyin uv *him*.

Dennis commented that Field apparently reworked this verse considerably more than most of his others; Dennis noted that to avoid being taken too seriously, Field inserted the following commentary in one of his columns written about the same time:

> Dialect verse is a precious fraud. Upon general principles it can be assumed, we think, that the writer of dialect verse is either a lazy poet—for dialect appears to be the natural refuge of the lazy, the doddering, and the inefficient—or the last flicker of a decaying intellect. Take it as we may, it is a sneaking but no less dangerous foe to our literature.

Field's attacks on the dangerous foes of literature were surely directed as much at what he considered his own weaknesses as at those of others. Significantly enough, in the weeks after this—particularly in May and June—he published absolutely no poetry. And then finally, with little or no warning, he climaxed the productions of what would later become known as his "Golden Year" with a solid week of nothing but poetry. For most readers, the variety—not to mention the output—was nothing short of mind-boggling. If there was a common linkage in this impressive medley, it was virtually impossible to find. Titles ranged from the dialect of "Professor Vere de Blau"—which appeared on the first day, July 15—to the expected adaptations such as Beranger's "To My Old Coat" and Horace's "Sailor and Shade." Included among them were Field's attempts at Alaskan balladry such as "The Wooing of the Southland" which rhythmically proclaimed the Southland's refusal to join the North in matrimony:

> The sea wails loud, and the sea wails long,
>   As the ages of waiting drift slowly by,
> But the sea shall sing no bridal song—
>   As well know you and I!

No doubt as far as Field's own directions were concerned, it was the poem appearing on the last day of the week—"The Biblio-maniac's Bride"—which told the most prophetic story. In this poem, Field humorously confessed his bibliomanic inclinations. If given his choice, Field declared, "I'd choose no folio tall, / But some octavo to rejoice."

> As plumb and pudgy as a snipe;
>   Well worth her weight in gold;
> Of honest, clean, conspicuous type
>   And *just* the size to hold!
>
> With such a volume for my wife
>   How should I keep and con!
> How like a dream should run my life
>   Unto its colophon!

In so writing, Field was, in fact, mentally preparing for his imminent departure for Europe—a trip to ease the anxiety of living in a city, even a country, where tradition indicated few artistic pathways. Although he would not leave until early October, as early as June 11, 1889 he wrote his friend Edward Cowen regarding his intended lodgings in London. "I want to get cheap but desirable quarters—a pleasant place, not fashionable, and *not* too far from the old-book shops." Amidst the book stalls of the older, well-assured world cultures, Field hoped to find guideposts which he could apply to his own predicament of not knowing what art, or, perhaps even he, himself, stood for in his society. In the meantime, he would put his immediate affairs in order.

Before leaving, Field hoped to publish two "Little Books." The first would be comprised of the poetry he was then turning out for the *Daily News* and the second would consist of his short stories, or tales, which he had been working on for the past five years. His previous publishing ventures had been admitted fiascoes, and Field wanted to guard against such events happening again. This time his writings would not be for the popular market, but rather would be for the express delectation of his personal friends and hoped-for acquaintances in the "select" literary circles. As Field wrote at the time:

> My wish has been—and my effort—to produce two thoroughly pretty books—handsomely printed upon the best handmade paper, with graceful dedications, colophons and all that sort of thing. I have an honest and earnest desire to show the world that a western man *can* devise a neat volume.

Twice previously when Field's writings had been gathered together for market publication, the approach and techniques of packaging had been considerably different to what he was this time attempting. A collection of ninety-four of his sketches from the Denver *Tribune* were published in the form of a small pamphlet called *The Tribune Primer* in 1882. But in the words of his brother, Roswell, "Eugene at that time thought nothing of the *Primer,* and, indeed, never sent me a copy."

Field's second venture fared little better. In 1887, he had tried desperately to get Edmund Clarence Stedman to write an introduction for a collection of his writings from "Sharps and Flats." Stedman, however, had politely but emphatically refused and the book—entitled *Culture's Garland* with the "garland" represented by a ring of sausages gracing the head of the "Chicago Dante"— was poorly received. Field himself realized that, in spite of moderate sales in the East, "Chicago folk [were] not ready to buy a work that satirized them so mercilessly." And by 1893, he would write to a friend that although "I am not ashamed of this little book, like the boy with the measles, I am sorry for it in spots."

Considering such obvious errors of judgment, then, Field exerted the greatest caution in preparing his "Little Books" before embarking for Europe. As early as March 10, 1889, he wrote B. H. Ticknor of Boston, the original publisher of *Culture's Garland,* asking him, "please send me that bundle of stories you have been keeping for me so long—I mean *my own* stories. I have made up my mind to rewrite them all." These were the rejected stories which Field had sent Ticknor along with the material which was eventually included in *Culture's Garland.* As Field had described them at the time:

> They are stories for young and old; perhaps I should say that they are (most of them) children's stories so written as to interest the old folk. I have made them as simple as I could and in many of them the fairy element predominates.

Although Field unquestionably spent some time in reworking his early stories and in writing new ones, he could never quite get rid of what he called the "intrusive rodent" obstacle. Time and again in these stories, readers would find dreamy-eyed mice talking to grandfather clocks ("The Mouse and the Moonbeam") or sprightly crickets and sparrows talking to little boys ("Rudolph and His King") or, to vary the theme, oysters seeking the advice of porpoises ("Margaret: A Pearl"). While just as typical was the phenomenon of mountains falling in love with oceans ("The Mountain and the Sea") or, as in "The Oak-Tree and the Ivy," the problems encountered when a loving, young ivy plant wrapped her tendrils around the trunk of a wise, old oak tree that happened, in turn, to be struck by lightning.

"Dear oak-tree, you are riven by the storm-king's thunder-bolt!" cried the ivy, in anguish.

"Ay," said the oak-tree, feebly, "my end has come; see, I am shattered and helpless."

"But I am unhurt," remonstrated the ivy, "and I will bind up your wounds and nurse you back to health and vigor."

And, indeed, the ivy did—by telling quaint stories to the oak tree which "she had learned from the crickets, the bees, the butter-flies, and the mice."

Of the twenty-one stories which appeared in Field's *Little Book of Profitable Tales,* all but six bore strong signs, in one way or another, of the "intrusive rodent." The remaining stories, which were understandably the most popular, were written in western dialect. Perhaps of these stories, the one which was the most pop-ular was that which seemingly departed the most from the others and, in so doing, came closest to bridging the limits of genteel de-corum. In "The Little Yaller Baby," Field told, in first-person narrative, the story of a "westerner" going by train to "Saint Louey." Although the man was notably insensitive when it came to dealing with the black porter (" 'Look a' hyar, Sam,' says I to the nigger, 'come hyar 'nd bresh me off ag'in!' "), he displayed admirable concern regarding the welfare of the little "yaller" baby. What soon became the apparent reason for the baby's looking so peculiar was that the child's mother had recently died and the dis-traught father had no way of providing it with nourishment. But

193

fortunately an unusual solution—or at least an unusual solution in terms of nineteenth-century literature—was found in the graciousness of another young traveler.

> What did the lady over the way do but lay her own sleepin' baby down on the seat beside her 'nd take Bill's little yaller baby 'nd hold it on one arm 'nd cover up its head 'nd her shoulder with a shawl, jist like she had done with the fat baby not long afore.

Another of Field's popular dialect series was the partially autobiographical tale which he published for the first time in his "Sharps and Flats" column for January 31, 1889. In "The Cyclopeedy," Field described the trials and tribulations of Leander Hobart in paying off his twenty-six-volume encyclopedia—letter by letter and "fiver" by "fiver." Finally, "one balmy day in the spring uv '87" when Leander's life "wuz a-ebbin' powerful fast," all of a sudden "ol' Leander riz up in bed 'nd sez, 'It's come!' "

> "What is it, Father?" asked his daughter Sarey, sobbin' like.
> "Hush," says the minister, solemnly; "he sees the shinin' gates uv the Noo Jerusalem."
> "No, no," cried the aged man; "it is the cyclopeedy—the letter **Z**—it's comin'!"

Fortunately for Field, however, Leander Hobart's lifelong predicament was one which he would no longer have to worry about. By mid-September, Field completed agreements with the University Press at Cambridge, Massachusetts for the limited editions of his *Little Book of Western Verse* and its companion, *A Little Book of Profitable Tales*. And on October 6, 1889—with a severe case of "nervous dyspepsia"—he and his family set sail for London. Field had scarcely time to get settled, however, before word started arriving on the high demand for his "Little Books." The original 114 subscribers had paid five dollars for each set. But in virtually no time at all, the price first doubled, then more than tripled as the demand for the limited copies soared spectacularly. Not surprisingly, by March 2 of the following year—with the going price marked at twenty-five dollars for any set which could be acquired—Field wrote his Cousin Julia that "I am sorry now that I limited the edition." But he then added more cheerfully, "a cheap edition will probably be brought out in the summer in time to catch the next Christmas-holiday trade."

Field's prophecy was accurate beyond his wildest dreams. The editors at Scribners issued the popular edition in time to attract the hoped-for holiday traffic. And with this event, there could no longer remain even the faintest doubt about the national status of Field's reputation. The bookdealer George M. Millard spoke incredulously of the extent of the success:

> I happen to know that he received a check for a few cents less than $2,000 as his royalties for six months on two volumes of his works. And that was exceptionally good—very large, as royalties go. There were more of his books sold that year than any other publication of that house.

Given such overwhelming good fortune, Field felt free to give full energies to his crusade for bettering the lot of Chicago culture. His fellow citizens' denial of a literary tradition—their attempts to *buy* culture without doing the necessary homework—had always seemed to Field a form of heresy. Before he had always ridiculed them for their false pretensions; now he saw clearly a new duty.

He would provide his readers—through the offerings in his "Sharps and Flats" column—with the necessary literary sustenance. They would no longer have to feel the cruel inferiority which he, himself, had felt with the rebuffs of such eastern critics as Edmund Clarence Stedman. If his fellow townsmen had neither the time nor inclination to do their essential homework, in London he would do it for them. He wrote his newspaper friend Charles Dennis that "every day I go upon a ramble, invariably through St. Martin's Lane (where Prout, Jerrold, Thackeray, and that coterie used to get convivial), down into the Strand or up byways into lanes and alleys where the musty book and print shops are." And he wrote Harriet Monroe's father, "I see by the papers that Chicago's population reaches a million! Can this be true? How proud we all are of that city, and why should we not try to make her proud of us?"

The way to "win" the city, Field now saw was not by mercilessly satirizing her cultural foibles—Field had already tried that in *Culture's Garland* and that had obviously failed—but by transforming the words of the literary "touchstones" into a language which could be readily understood. But this could not be done through the "precious fraud" of dialect verse. Rather, he could use direct translations and paraphrasings to capture the "spirit" of the letter. If Field did continue, however, from time to time to write in dialect verse or resort to the easy sentimentalism of his nursery rhymes—which he once confidentially referred to as "mother rot" —this was merely secondary to his greater purpose of providing the essential literary roots. In words clearly indicative of his emerging self-conception of this role, he wrote to his old friend and rival, Edmund Clarence Stedman, in 1889:

> I am neither a poet nor an author. I am simply a newspaper
> man, seeking to do somewhat towards improving newspaper litera-
> ture. I am a thistle, standing in a bleak but fertile prairie; if the
> high winds scatter my seed hither and thither, I shall be content,
> for then other thistles will issue therefrom and make the prairie
> beautiful after a fashion. But, presently advancing culture will
> root up the thistles and then more beautiful flowers will bloom in
> our stead; that conviction pleases me most.

Field, for his part, would do everything in his power to help
the scattering process. Upon his return from London, he published in rapid succession: *Echoes from the Sabine Farm* (a collection of paraphrases of Horatian odes), *With Trumpet and Drum*
(a collection of verse similar to that previously issued), *The Second
Book of Verse* (still more verse along this line), *The Holy Cross
and Other Tales* (additional stories of the "intrusive rodent" variety), and *Love Songs of Childhood* (an apparent attempt to
boost his standing amongst the nation's mothers). All these books
were published between the time of Field's return from Europe in
1891 and 1894. Their publishing histories matched those of his "Little Books"; they were issued first in limited editions and then in
widely acclaimed popular editions. With few exceptions, all his
writings could be found originally in his daily contributions to
the Chicago *Record*.

This pattern was directly in line with the goals he had set for
himself while still in London. In writing Harriet Monroe, at that
time, he had declared:

> If I have an honest purpose it is to give lie to the absurd heresy
> that a newspaper writer cannot write literature for his newspaper.

It is with this ambition in view that I have put aside all pecuniary considerations and given my work freely and cheerfully to the newspaper. So little do I regret this alleged folly and so much in earnest am I in it that I shall probably continue in this way of doing to the end of my life.

If Field had changed during his stay abroad in terms of his renewed dedication and commitment to his work, so too had Chicago changed during this period in terms of the city's sense of worldly importance and self-dedication. The picking of Chicago's Jackson Park in 1890 as the location for the World's Columbian Exposition of 1893 had generated enormous energies on behalf of her citizens. Before the Fair's closing, in the fall of 1893, more than $19 million would be spent in such extravagant preparations as the complete engineering of the Midway Plaisance for The Bazaar of Nations—where "Little Egypt" performed her daring dances—and the building of a giant pier which afforded a smooth-water harbor for the plentiful marine exhibits. Of the total $19 million spent, Chicago's own citizens could boast that they had contributed no less than $5.6 million to the spectacular event.

Charles Dennis recalled Field's fascination with the majestic "White City." He remembered that Field was given "an unlimited license from the management of the *Daily News* to entertain distinguished visitors at its expense how and when he pleased." Often, recalled Dennis, Field could be seen in the evenings with out-of-town guests amidst the festive surroundings of the Midway.

Beyond sheer entertainment, however, the Fair provided Field with an opportunity to expand upon his own literary designs. When Mary Hartwell Catherwood entered into lively debate with Hamlin Garland during the Fair's Literary Congress, Field joyfully came to the rescue of what he termed Mrs. Catherwood's "embroidery needle and lance" as opposed to Garland's "dung fork" of literary realism. "Mr. Garland's heroes sweat and do not wear socks," protested Field, "and his heroines eat cold huckleberry pie and are so unfeminine as not to call a cow 'he.'"

Before Field finished his remarks, a majority of six columns of "Sharps and Flats" had been devoted to the celebrated fray. What most irked Field was Garland's alleged confession that one of his purposes was to subvert the Grand Republican Party. "Then, too," added Field, "he would burn up all fairy tales and ghost stories—just think of that!" And for Field, the thought of the latter was simply too painful for his romantic spirit to endure.

When Field's post-London poetry first appeared, his readers were surprised to find even more of it devoted to the paraphrasings of Horace than before. His first book upon his return, *Echoes from the Sabine Farm,* was devoted exclusively to such work. Lest his readers become overly concerned, he explained his services in no uncertain terms. Field was doing for them what the eastern literati, the James Russell Lowells, refused to do with their unsubtle offerings of pre-packaged and pre-digested culture. Field explained that while "others" had attempted to set up Horace "as a kind of scarecrow to shoo schoolboys in terror away from classic pursuit, I choose a better part." Field reacted with a vengeance against all the hypocrisy of his own upbringing—the stodginess of his New England ancestry which had forced him to swallow whole the harsh instruction they foisted upon him. He would, in no way, allow himself to fall prey to such pandering. "I am anxious to have it understood," wrote Field, "that in my work of paraphrasing [one] purpose has been held steadfastly in mind—to give Horace to my readers in the garb and vernacular of the present time." He then added:

> Horace belongs to us, to this age, to this century, to this decade, to this year—yes, to this very day! And he belongs to every people that appreciates the geniality, the poetry, the charity and the gracious, saving frailty of human nature.

Should his readers still find difficulty in understanding what Field was getting at, they had merely to compare Field's Horatian translations with those of a "reputable" scholar such as Sir Theodore Martin. Martin's version of "Persicos, odi" went as follows:

> Persia's pomp, my boy, I hate,
> No coronals of flowerets rare
> For me on bark of linden plait,
> Nor seek thou, to discover where
> The lush rose lingers late.

Field's "no holds barred" approach went in this manner:

> Boy, I detest the Persian pomp;
> I hate those linden-bark devices;
> As for roses, holy Moses!
> They can't be got at living prices!

Those who quibbled with Field's accuracy somehow missed the point. As Field aptly explained, "we might haggle forever about what Horace meant nineteen hundred years ago; [but] what does he mean to-day?"

If Field's tales of fancy, on the other hand, were plagued by

intrusive mice, moths, and other eighteenth-century creatures without the benefit of present-day garb, this was an inconsistency with
which most of Field's friends and readers learned to live. There was
really no perceptible change between those stories Field sent T. H.
Ticknor in 1887 and those he wrote shortly before his death nearly
a decade later. Perhaps more than anything else, these stories
indicated that beneath his bravado Field was still plagued by all
the fears of the rebellious schoolboy. It was one thing to poke fun
at the false standards of the culture bearers of the "Porkopolis"
or the pretentiousness of the East Coast literati, but it was another thing to create one's *own* standards of literary excellence.
When it came to this, Field yielded scarcely an inch from the traditional forms. The children's poetry which he dashed off in time
for his newspaper deadlines could be easily enough dismissed as
part of the hazards of the profession. If they were criticized at all,
they were usually criticized with the kind of sympathetic understanding which seemed implicit in the very poetry itself. As one
critic noted in discussing the "People's Poets"—Field and James
Whitcomb Riley—"The world does not say of them that they are
brilliant beyond all other craftsmen. It contents itself with loving
them."

Because of this attitude, Field once told Hamlin Garland that
he never put a high estimate on his verse. "That it's popular," he
proclaimed, "is because my sympathies and the public's happen to
run on parallel lines just now. That's all." His stories, on the other
hand, were something else and they would probably never have
sold very well had it not been for his other writings. But these
were the writings which Field slaved over. "The Werewolf," which
was published posthumously in *The Second Book of Verse,* was

completely rewritten at least seven times. Slason Thompson remembered that Field, in writing this story about a girl who falls in love with a werewolf, was uncommonly "finicky and beset with doubts as to the use of words and phrases." But in spite of such efforts, Thompson noted, "the result [was] a marvellous piece of technicality [sic] perfect archaic old English mosaic"—and disappointingly devoid of soul.

> Then, ah, then in very truth there was great joy, and loud were the acclaims, while, beautiful in her trembling pallor, Yseult was led unto her home, where the people set about to give great feast to do her homage, for the werewolf was dead, and *she* it was that had slain him.

Despite such disastrous results, Field was convinced that his most lasting reputation would rest first on his stories and second on his satire. Actually, the exact opposite was the case. Besides, no matter what else Field did, he was always remembered most of all as the "Children's Laureate"—the man who dipped his pen into the "inkstand of the heart."

When Field was persuaded in 1893 to sign up with the lecture circuits—first with Bill Nye and James Whitcomb Riley and later as Mark Twain's successor with George Washington Cable—it was invariably his children's verse which his audience most demanded. A handbill for the Fred Felham Agency proclaimed:

> Mr. Field has become widely known through his "Sharps and Flats" column in the Chicago *Daily Record*, and his translations from Horace have also made him familiar to the public, but it is through his exquisite poems of children and child-life that his name has become a household word, both East and West.

And for those who came to hear him there was one poem in particular which could never be ignored in an evening's entertainment—Field's "Little Boy Blue." When he performed in Chicago in 1893, the newspaper account reported that "The audience was there to see the man who drove the pen that, dipped in tears and tenderness, lined the 'Little Boy Blue.'" And when he spoke in Boston the New York *Tribune* account reported that "The women —they were mostly women present—laughed and cried, smiled and applauded and hung upon this Western Yankee's deep tones." Adding that, when it came to reading "Little Boy Blue," Field gave "plenty of emotion."

Occasionally, but not very often, Field would challenge—but never violate—the refinements of his audience. In New Orleans, in 1894, when Field reportedly "stood forth like a gleam of sunshine in the general gloom and dullness of the lenten season," he recited the story of "The Little Yaller Baby." With Field's "delicacy of handling of what would [have] otherwise [been] risqué . . . probably the general opinion awarded the palm to his recital of [this] story."

Invariably, however, during these performances Field was billed as the "author of 'Little Boy Blue,'" and after his death there was the understandable speculation as to what specific incident had inspired the magic words. Apparently, while he was living it had been considered too delicate a subject for public debate. After all, there had been the time when Field had acted "manifestly disturbed" when asked to recite "Little Boy Blue" at a banquet in New York. A member of the audience at the time remembered that after Field began, each line fell weaker than the next. "Finally, he stopped. 'Gentlemen, I cannot go on,' he said. 'Tonight is the anniversary of his death.'"

But the speculation remained . . . whose death? Most felt it must have been Field's son Melvin, who died while the Fields were in Europe and precipitated their return to America. But as Charles Dennis and others pointed out, Melvin had, in fact, died almost two and a half years *after* "Little Boy Blue" first appeared. Others, such as editor Melville Stone, said that it must have been the infant son who died while the Fields were living in St. Joseph. But in addition to never having grown old enough to play with little toy dogs and soldiers—he died at three months—this child's death took place almost twelve years before the poem actually made its appearance in Thompson's *America*. The "Unsinkable" Molly Brown, on the other hand, distinctly remembered that Julia, herself, had recited the poem on the death of her "little son" while living in Denver. But, of course, there was no son who died while the Fields were in Denver, and the poem was still years away from its creation.

Francis Wilson had once tried unsuccessfully to reduce the confusion. In writing his 1898 account of *The Eugene Field I Knew,* he explained that " 'Little Boy Blue' [was] popularly thought to have been suggested by the loss of one of Field's children. Such, however, as he has repeatedly declared, was not the case." But then Julia, in going over the manuscript, crossed out the last line with the curious notation: "I have reason for not wanting this so stated." And whatever the reason, Julia's suggestion was apparently sufficient to convince Wilson to delete the objectionable line from the manuscript. Besides, Julia was known to have been particularly emotional when it came to the subject. And on at least one occasion, tears had streamed her face when, in spite of her objections, Field had persisted in reciting "Little Boy Blue."

She later blurted out, in apparent apology, that "Eugene wrote those lines when our baby died."

Charles Dennis obviously thought most such statements and speculations were sentimental and foolish. In 1924, he tried to set the matter straight once and for all by stating adamantly that "Field never intimated to me at the time the poem was written or at any other time that it was anything more than the product of his imagination."

Finally, in 1944, long after the commotion had subsided and "Little Boy Blue" was virtually forgotten by a majority of Americans, so weighty an explanation was provided as to cast serious doubt on all others. Charles Newton French, a Chicago lawyer and poet, declared in a privately printed leaflet, that, in truth, *he* was the author of the original version of "Little Boy Blue."

According to his account, on September 6, 1884, French had sent a poem entitled "Boy Blue" to the Chicago *Daily News* and received no response to either his poem or his enclosed letter. Then, in 1891, after Field's own "Little Boy Blue" had boosted his reputation to national status, French, in search of an explanation, made a trip to the *Daily News*. Regarding the trip, French later recalled that "by arrangement with Miss Werner, secretary to Victor Lawson, the publisher, I met Field and Thompson. At the request of the latter, I recited my poem; neither of them denied my authorship."

French's poem, as included in his 1944 leaflet, differed noticeably but certainly not drastically from Field's own "Little Boy Blue." French's version had, indeed, a "Little Boy Blue" who one night toddled off "to his tiny bed" after placing a "little toy dog" and its companion soldier on a nearby shelf. And, as in the more

popular version, after the little boy was awakened by an "angel
song," the little toys, though covered with dust, remained "true."
In French's account:

> That was the time that Little Boy Blue
> Kissed them and put them there.

Furthermore, years later French approached Charles Dennis
when he was editor emeritus at the *Daily News*.

> We examined each version separately, then compared them.
> He [Dennis] noted that the Field version, by its line, "In the dust
> of that little chair," employs a demonstrative adjective, "that,"
> without an antecedent, a fact tending to prove that Field had a
> portion, but only a portion, of my text before him when in one
> night he produced his version.

And notably, in Field's version, there is, indeed, no mention
of any chair before it becomes "that" chair in the third from the
last line. French then concluded his remarks:

> Before departing, my distinguished visitor [Dennis] auto-
> graphed to me a copy of his well written Field biography, stated
> that I should write my story, and expressed a wish for a copy of
> my text for study. After that time some correspondence of impor-
> tance passed between us. More recently his useful life ceased.

Unfortunately, in terms of verification, French did not publish his views on the *real* "Little Boy Blue" until after Dennis's
death. But there could be, in any case, little doubt but that Dennis,

in his later years, grew to have serious doubts about the accuracy of his own and other such works. Dennis, in his 1935 biography of *Victor Lawson: His Time and His Work,* makes the curious remark that "so much has been written about Field that little remains to be written save an adequate biography." And this from the man who—a decade before—had, himself, written a 350-page "study."

Even in his original writing, Dennis had some indication that Field did not always adhere to the strictest ethics in preparing his material. After Field's death, Dennis had received an unusual letter from George Vinton who once worked under Field on the Denver *Tribune.* Vinton, who was then an elocution teacher in Chicago, claimed:

> The "Yaller Baby" story was written by me. I gave the story to Ballantyne [Field's managing editor] to give to Field, expecting to be given credit for it. Field changed it a little, putting in the coloured porter, which spoiled it for me. The rest was all mine.

By including this letter, Dennis apparently hoped to preserve the sanctity of Field's reputation. For, in so doing, he added that this was "the only charge of the sort that I ever heard associated with his work." Most likely, Dennis was aware of other "indiscretions" but he probably considered them within the limits of journalistic fair play. After all, Field's numerous false attributions to others—such as the parody of Riley which he attributed to William Dean Howells—were widely appreciated by all, save Howells, and fully recorded in Dennis's own study. And even if Field had, in fact, "borrowed" the "Yaller Baby" story, he *had* altered it in some degree. Dennis, therefore, concluded: "I am convinced that he regarded 'The Little Yaller Baby' as wholly his own after he had carefully recast it."

Perhaps, then, in recasting such pieces as "The Little Yaller Baby" and "Little Boy Blue" Field was, in a sense, merely performing his duties as a newspaper editor—that is, he was artfully preparing the copy he received to meet the demands of a newspaper audience. Surely, at least in his own view, he was neither a poet nor an author but "simply a newspaper man, seeking to do somewhat towards improving newspaper literature." There was hardly an individual, in this regard, who would have denied his excellence.

Perhaps the most serious charge which could be brought against Field was that he became the almost unknowing victim of his own prophecy. Scattering his seed upon the "bleak but fertile prairie," Field very nearly uprooted himself—a "thistle"—for the sake of what he considered the more important flowering of the "advancing culture."

Field believed that the advancing culture could grow only in a climate where people were aware of their literary roots. But—in a society where most schooling conspired against *real* awareness— this knowledge had to come through people such as himself. Field, in seeking out his own roots—amidst the bookstalls of St. Martin's Lane at first, and later in Boston and New Orleans—inadvertently weakened himself for the purposes of his greater task. The more familiar he became with the traditional cultures, the less willing he became to make the necessary translations.

After his return from London, he spent considerably fewer hours at his downtown office. Instead of returning to the *Daily News* after an evening at the theater, as had been his previous practice, he used the pretense of his "nervous dyspepsia" as an excuse to return home to bed and there, amongst his books, read and write until early morning. Charles Dennis remembered that Field "during the last four years of his life did his writing at home and his son Fred [Daisy] drew a small weekly wage from the newspaper [for carrying] his father's manuscript to the office."

Even when Field did venture downtown, his forays more often than not led him to the "Saints and Sinners Corner" at McClurg's bookstore. The book browsers who frequented this particular section of rare and old books grew accustomed to seeing their names appear in some jesting manner in Field's columns. William F. Poole, in particular, who for years was executive head of the Chicago Public Library and later founded the Newberry Library, found his name indecorously linked with the buffooneries of witchcraft and baseball. Other such honored "members" included: George Armour, Ben T. Cable, Charles Barnes, as well as the Reverends Frank W. Gunsaulus and Frank M. Bristol. The name itself—"Saints and Sinners"—derived from Field's mischievous play on the occupations of his bookish friends. Although there were, in fact, no formal meetings of this group, their fictional proceedings were widely publicized in the *Daily News.*

Not surprisingly, the "Sharps and Flats" of the later years grew increasingly dissimilar from those of the earlier period. Instead of satirical comments on the clash of Chicago's cultural and political forces, readers found obscure bibliographic references to literature they neither understood nor cared about. As such, it failed to either instruct the citizens of Chicago on how they might laughingly cope with their political dilemmas or, even more seriously, learn to cultivate their literary "prairie." By 1894, Field explained to a friend:

. . . in confidence I'll tell you that I'm tired of writing about people and things that do not interest me. How can I possibly enjoy dealing with the cheap ephemeral cattle in Chicago ward-politics? Bah! Someday I may be able to indulge my taste for work of a better character.

By the next year, 1895, Field was hard at work on two volumes—*The House* and *The Love Affairs of a Bibliomaniac*—both in serial in his "Sharps and Flats" column. Both strictly avoided the dilemmas of Chicago's ward politics and, rather, heralded the less politically engaging pastimes of suburban living and book collecting. If *The House*—with its humorous accounts of wallpapering, negotiating with plumbers, and renovating hardwood floors —stood for one level of escape, *The Love Affairs* carried this retreat one step further into the hushed atmosphere of the library. Here one found Field's random thoughts on the pleasures of book-hunting as told from the perspective of a gentleman-collector recounting the conquests of his all-embracing passion.

For many, very many years I have walked in a pleasant garden, enjoying sweet odors and soothing spectacles. And now it is my purpose to walk that pleasant garden once more, inviting you to bear me company and to share with me what satisfaction may accrue from an old man's return to old-time places and old-time loves.

This final walk of Field's was designed to picture the "delights, adventures, and misadventures, connected with bibliomania." As such, it described with mock, yet subtle, seriousness the unique delights of reading in bed, the relation between the baldness and intellectuality, and, ultimately, the intoxicating pleasures of old and treasured books. "Have you ever come out of the thick, smoky atmosphere of the town," asked the collector, "into the fragrant, gracious atmosphere of the library? If you have," he added, "you know how grateful the change is . . . nothing else is so quieting to the nerves, so conducive to physical health, and so quick to restore a lively flow of the spirits."

Amongst the bibliomaniac's loves (ranging from Hans Christian Andersen to Villon and Boccaccio) the collector's first love was revealed as that "curious little thin book in faded blue board covers"— *The New England Primer*. Field's initial act of journalistic rebellion—the parody of the *Primer* as found in the Denver *Tribune*—was now elevated by time, tradition, and geography to a place of veneration. So complete was Field's fictional retreat, that, in the words of the aged collector, "right truly can I say that from the springtime day sixty-odd years ago, when first my heart went out in love to this little book, no change of scene or of custom, no allurement of fashion has abated that love." Books were, according to Field, dependable and did not change. But people were otherwise. They might laugh and cry, but inevitably they grew old and died.

Field finished the nineteenth installment of *The Love Affairs* on Saturday afternoon, November 2, 1895. According to his brother, Roswell, there was but one chapter remaining before the work would be completed. This final chapter was to describe the old bibliomaniac's final rewards—his pleasant death after coming across, at long last, a priceless copy of his revered Horace. Two days later, just before dawn on November 4—with that final chapter still unwritten—Eugene Field suddenly died.

Piled about him—on shelves and tucked into remote corners— were the splendid treasures of his book-filled garden. Too delicate to grow on a windy prairie, Field had hoarded them in an artificial greenhouse—their pleasures to be savored by a select few. By mid-morning on November 4, with the sun high over Lake Michigan, shocked reporters from the city's newsrooms gathered in silent awe. Beside them and above them were the Canton flannel elephant with the scarlet and gold howdah, the strange pewter dishes, and the heaps and heaps of old, old books.

Chicago Historical Society

Field's move to the suburbs provided a necessary relief from city tensions. Pictured here, Field and Julia, Buena Park, 1894.

Chicago Historical Society

Chicago Historical Society

At his office at the *Daily News*, Field and Charles Dennis compared newspaper clippings of Field's "Little Boy Blue" with James Russell Lowell's "St. Michael the Weigher."

Denver Public Library

Most popular with Field's newspaper fans were his trips to the nursery. Pictured here, Julia with "Posy" and "Sister Girl."

Denver Public Library

Amidst the book stalls of the older, well-
assured world cultures, Field hoped to find
guideposts for his own position in American society.

After *Culture's Garland* appeared, Field realized "Chicago folk were not ready to buy a work that satirized them so mercilessly." Pictured here, Field, Trotty, and Chicago friends.

Denver Public Library

Denver Public Library

In London, Field wrote Dennis that "every day I go upon a ramble . . . down into the Strand or up byways into lanes and alleys where the musty book and print shops are." Pictured here, Julia and Field, London, 1890.

Chicago Historical Society

Field joined his fellow citizens in celebration at the opening of the World's Columbian Exposition of 1893.

Denver Public Library

Field met with the "People's Poets"—James Whitcomb Riley and Bill Nye—for this formal portrait. Indianapolis, 1886.

Chicago Historical Society

The author of "Little Boy Blue" found time to read his poetry to the neighborhood children. Buena Park, *c.* 1894.

Field posed beside this tree in his backyard at Buena Park, *c.* 1895.

Chicago Historical Society

Slason Thompson complained that the photographs taken a few months before Field's death were "ghastly travesties on the nomadic character of his domestic arrangements." Pictured here,

Field, Trotty, and Pinny. Buena Park, July 1895.

Denver Public Library

Denver Public Library

Field and friends. Buena Park, July 1895.

The Eugene Field House

Field was hard at work on the final pages of *The Love Affairs of a Biblio-maniac* when he passed away the morning of November 4, 1895.

Epilogue

The Eugene Field House

After her husband's death, Julia lamented that "more houses in this country need to be homes." Pictured here, Julia with Sister Girl and Posy at the time of Trotty's wedding, October 16, 1902, exactly twenty-seven years to the day after Julia and Eugene's wedding in St. Joseph in 1873.

On the eve of her seventy-eighth birthday, in 1934, Julia Field granted a rare interview. Described by the visiting reporter as one of the "world's true mothers," Julia sat ensconced amongst the few family objects remaining—mostly valued, first-edition books and family portraits. As Julia told the reporter, times had seriously changed since her husband had first captured the nation's enthusiastic regard. "I don't deny that Carrie Chapman Catts are important," proclaimed Julia in obvious dismay, "but more houses in this country need to be homes."

Julia was well aware that Americans of the Thirties were no longer content to focus their undivided attentions on the home values represented by Field's sentimental verse. Since his death, in fact, Americans had been continually breaking down and reworking traditional family patterns. On the advice of celebrated spokeswomen—such as Charlotte Perkins Gilman and Carrie Chapman

Catt—women, in increasing numbers, had stepped out of the home to take jobs in the open market. They were told—and sometimes urged—that it was their inherent right to assume roles equal to their husbands' in the larger society. Eventually, in the Thirties, such proddings became more than mere advice. Despite fierce competition between men and women for the few remaining jobs, in many instances the only hope for domestic security existed when both husband and wife worked. And these same women—whose very mothers had provided the mainstay of Field's reputation while he lived—now found little time or desire to attend literary lyceums and shed unchecked tears over the fate of "Little Boy Blue." In the midst of the Depression, they had their own earthly fates to worry about.

Women, perhaps sooner than men, became aware of the inadequacies of such easy sentimentalizing. All of the leading preservationists—save Molly Brown—were men; and these were generally Field's personal male friends and fellow journalists. As such, they exerted tremendous influence over the nation's channels of communication. While the rest of the country grew weary with war and financial burden, this handful of men increasingly championed the reputation of Eugene Field. The monuments they looked after and the books they wrote invariably received full coverage in the daily news. And Field's name, in the process, became greatly inflated. But by the late Thirties, when these men either died or retired from their positions of influence, the reputation of Eugene Field followed closely thereafter.

Finally, when word came from Tomahawk, Wisconsin, on June 8, 1936, that Julia Field had passed away, there was understandably little commotion. The single-column obituary in the New York *Times* noted that until one month prior to her death, many of Field's former acquaintances had not realized that Julia was still alive. Then it had become publicized, through the benefactor of Field's St. Louis house, Jesse P. Henry, that Julia was indeed alive but in a great deal of trouble. Recently she had suffered a series of heart attacks in trying to save her 150-acre farm from foreclosure. Most of Julia's property, which relatives had estimated at $200,000, had been lost in Chicago real estate during the Depression. Ultimately, with virtually all her resources depleted, Julia had been refused even a modest loan by the Home Owners Loan Corporation of America. The farm, to which Julia had reportedly fled nearly a decade earlier with Little Boy Blue's baby shoes, was now, itself, the victim of financial privation. Yet, even at this late hour, all was not lost. There were still those who cared and remembered. The members of Field's Knox College fraternity, Phi Delta Theta, heard the plea and came forth with a check for $2,600 which adequately covered the mortgage and several small items.

Then, a month later, following her fifth heart attack, Julia died. Her body was taken by train to Kenilworth where she was buried beside her husband in the tomb at the Church of the Holy Comforter.

Interestingly enough, neither Julia's death in 1936 nor Charles Newton French's 1944 account of "Little Boy Blue" provided sufficient impetus to serve final rites to the little toy dog and his companion soldier. Their vigil, even today, is faithfully guarded by a determined few. In Denver, if Molly Brown's "Lapin Agile" is now closed to the public, there is, in any case, a recently dedicated "Field Library" providing homage to his lasting influence. And in St. Louis, not far from the base of the 630-foot-high Gateway Arch, the Eugene Field House stands open for visitors and apparently unperturbed by either the earlier attacks of William Marion Reedy or the more recent push of urban renewal.

St. Joseph and Chicago tell similar stories. In St. Joseph, if the Lover's Lane—which Field once praised from London as that place of "leafy aisles"—is now a fashionable, but unheralded, suburban street, there is, nonetheless, a handsome statue of "Little Boy Blue" at the public library. And in Chicago, the school children, whose teachers may never mention Eugene Field, still daily pass by the "Dream Lady" memorial on their way to the animal house at Lincoln Park Zoo.

For those who do remember Field, the mists of time and distance have largely transformed his rich and shimmery career into a softer, more neutral cast. Much that Field wrote has, for all practical purposes, been lost forever. His journalistic pen was too facile, too closely tuned to the events of the day, to be captured by critic, biographer, or historic preservationist. Of all Field's writing, only a few lines remain for public observance—usually chiseled high above a schoolhouse door or placed in the remote corner of a public library. The rest, like so much summer lightning, has long since disappeared from view.

Bibliography

MANUSCRIPT COLLECTIONS

American Antiquarian Society, Worcester, Miscellaneous Collection.

Brown University, Eugene Field Papers.

Library of Congress, Eugene Field Papers.

Denver Public Library, Eugene Field Collection.

Harvard University, The Harvard College Library, Eugene Field Papers.

Henry E. Huntington Library, Eugene Field Papers.

Indiana University, The Lilly Library, Eugene Field Papers.

Jones Library, Amherst, Eugene Field Collection.

Knox College, Eugene Field Collection.

Missouri Historical Society, Eugene Field Papers.

Newberry Library, Chicago, Eugene Field Papers.

New York Public Library, The Henry W. and Albert A. Berg Collection. Astor, Lenox and Tilden Foundations.

New York Public Library, Francis Wilson Papers, Manuscripts and Archives Division. Astor, Lenox and Tilden Foundations.

St. John's Seminary, Eugene Field Papers.

St. Joseph Public Library, Eugene Field Papers.

State University of New York at Buffalo, Lockwood Memorial Library, Eugene Field Papers.

University of Chicago, The University of Chicago Library, Harriet Monroe Personal Papers.

University of Illinois at Chicago Circle, The Franklin J. Meine Collection.

University of Texas at Austin, Humanities Research Center, Eugene Field Papers.

University of Virginia, Alderman Library, Eugene Field Papers.

Washington University, Washington University Libraries, William K. Bixby Collection.

Yale University, Beinecke Rare Book and Manuscript Library, Eugene Field Papers.

NEWSPAPERS

Chicago Daily News, Chicago, Illinois.

Chicago Morning News, Chicago, Illinois.

Chicago Record, Chicago, Illinois.

Chicago Tribune, Chicago, Illinois.

Denver Tribune, Denver, Colorado.

Kansas City Times, Kansas City, Missouri.

New York Times, New York, New York.

St. Joseph Gazette, St. Joseph, Missouri.

St. Louis Times-Journal, St. Louis, Missouri.

✦ Bibliography ✦

PERIODICALS

America, Chicago, Illinois.

The Atlantic Monthly, Boston, Massachusetts.

The Book Buyer, New York, New York.

The Cornhill Booklet, Boston, Massachusetts.

The Knox Alumnus, Galesburg, Illinois.

Ladies' Home Journal, Philadelphia, Pennsylvania.

Leslie's Weekly, New York, New York.

McClure's, New York, New York.

The Mirror Pamphlets, St. Louis, Missouri.

Nation, New York, New York.

North American Review, New York, New York.

Our Day: The Altruistic Review, Boston, Massachusetts.

Scribner's, New York, New York.

St. Nicholas, New York, New York.

BOOKS

Andreas, A. T. *History of Chicago*. 3 vols. Chicago, 1886.

Andrews, Wayne. *Battle for Chicago*. New York, 1946.

Arps, Louis Ward. *Denver in Slices*. Denver, 1959.

Asbury, Herbert. *Gem of the Prairie: An Informal History of the Chicago Underworld*. New York, 1940.

Banta, Clara. *Eugene Field: The Story of His Life for Children*. Kansas City, 1898.

Below, Ida Comstock. *Eugene Field in His Home*. New York, 1898.

Birdsall, William W. *Literature of America and Our Favorite Authors*. Philadelphia, 1898.

Blodgett, Frances E. and Andrew B. *The Blodgett Second Reader.* Boston, 1905.

Bross, William. *Chicago and the Sources of Her Past and Future Growth.* Chicago, 1880.

Broun, Heywood and Leech, Margaret. *Anthony Comstock: Roundsman of the Lord.* New York, 1927.

Buder, Stanley. *Pullman: An Experiment in Industrial Order and Community Planning.* New York, 1967.

Burt, Mary E. and Cable, Mary B. *The Eugene Field Book.* New York, 1898.

Comstock, Anthony. *Traps for the Young.* Cambridge, 1967 reprint.

Davis, C. C. *Olden Times in Colorado.* Los Angeles, 1916.

Dedmon, Emmett. *Fabulous Chicago.* New York, 1953.

Dennis, Charles H. *Eugene Field's Creative Years.* New York, 1924.

————. *Victor Lawson: His Time and His Work.* Chicago, 1935.

Dreiser, Theodore. *A Book About Myself.* New York, 1922.

Duffey, Bernard. *The Chicago Renaissance in American Letters.* East Lansing, Michigan, 1954.

Duncan, Hugh D. *Culture and Democracy: The Struggle for Form in Society and Architecture in Chicago and the Middle West during the Life and Times of Louis H. Sullivan.* Totowa, New Jersey, 1965.

————. *The Rise of Chicago as a Literary Center from 1885 to 1920.* Totowa, New Jersey, 1964.

Elson, Ruth M. *Guardians of Tradition: American Schoolbooks of the Nineteenth Century.* Lincoln, Nebraska, 1964.

Field, Eugene. *My Book.* Privately printed in St. Louis, 1905.

————. *The Clink of Ice.* Chicago, 1905.

————. *The Complete Tribune Primer.* Minneapolis, 1967 reprint.

————. *Culture's Garland: being memoranda of the gradual rise of litera-*

ture, art, music and society in Chicago and other western ganglia. Boston, 1887.

————. *Florence Bardsley's Story.* Chicago, 1897.

————. *Flowers from Eugene Field.* Boston, 1906.

————. *The Holy Cross and Other Tales.* Cambridge, 1893.

————. *The House: An Episode in the Lives of Reuben Baker, Astronomer, and of His Wife Alice.* New York, 1896.

————. *John Smith, U.S.A.* Chicago, 1905.

————. *Libidinous Facetiae.* Privately printed in Chicago, 1903.

————. *A Little Book of Profitable Tales.* Chicago, 1889.

————. *A Little Book of Tribune Verse.* Denver, 1901.

————. *A Little Book of Western Verse.* Chicago, 1889.

————. *The Love Affairs of a Bibliomaniac.* New York, 1896.

————. *Love Songs of Childhood.* New York, 1894.

————. *Lullaby Land.* New York, 1897.

————. *The Poems of Eugene Field.* New York, 1920.

————. *A Second Book of Verse.* Chicago, 1892.

————. *Sharps and Flats.* 2 vols. New York, 1901.

————. *Songs and Other Verse.* New York, 1896.

————. *The Stars.* New York, 1901.

————. *The Tribune Primer.* Denver, 1881.

————. *With Trumpet and Drum.* New York, 1892.

————. *In Wink-Away Land.* Chicago, 1905.

Field, Eugene and Field, Roswell M. *Echoes from the Sabine Farm.* Chicago, 1892.

Fisher, Harry W. *Abroad with Mark Twain and Eugene Field.* New York, 1922.

French, Charles Newton. *Story of Little Boy Blue.* Privately printed in Chicago, 1944.

◆§ *Bibliography* §◆

A Gentleman About Town (pseudonym). *Immortalia*. No place, 1927.

Ginger, Ray, ed. *American Social Thought*. New York, 1961.

Harris, Alice L. *Eugene Field Reader*. New York, 1905.

Hart, James D. *The Popular Book: A History of America's Literary Taste*. New York, 1950.

Howard, O. O., ed. *Views of Denver Colorado*. Denver, 1889.

Ingersoll, Ernest. *Crest of the Continent*. Chicago, 1885.

Inter Ocean news staff, eds. *Chicago's First Half Century*. Chicago, 1883.

Johnson, Herrick. *A Plain Talk About the Theater*. New York, 1882.

Knight, Grant C. *The Critical Period in American Literature*. Chapel Hill, North Carolina, 1951.

Legman, Gershon. *The Horn Book: Studies in Erotic Folklore and Bibliography*. New York, 1964.

Lindsey, Almont. *The Pullman Strike: The Story of a Unique Experiment and of a Great Labor Upheaval*. Chicago, 1942.

Loth, David. *The Erotic in Literature: A historical survey of pornography as delightful as it is indiscreet*. New York, 1961.

Lowell, James Russell. *The Complete Poetical Works of James Russell Lowell*. Boston and New York, 1896.

McVicker, J. H. *The Press, the Pulpit and the Stage*. Chicago, 1883.

Marcus, Steven. *The Other Victorians: A Study of Sexuality and Pornography in Mid-Nineteenth-Century England*. New York, 1966.

Martin, Theodore. *The Works of Horace*. Edinburgh and London, 1888.

Masters, Edgar Lee. *The Tale of Chicago*. New York, 1933.

Meeker, Arthur. *Chicago with Love: A Polite and Personal History*. New York, 1955.

Mott, Frank Luther. *American Journalism*. New York, 1962.

———. *Golden Multitudes: The Story of Best Sellers in the United States*. New York, 1947.

Nolan, Jeannette C. *The Gay Poet: The Story of Eugene Field.* New York, 1967.

Papashvily, Helen Waite. *All the Happy Endings.* New York, 1956.

Pierce, Bessie Louise, ed. *As Others See Chicago: Impressions of Visitors, 1673–1933.* Chicago, 1933.

Pierce, Frederick C. *Field Genealogy.* Chicago, 1901.

Prade, Ruth L., ed. *Debs and the Poets.* Pasadena, California, 1920.

Rugoff, Milton. *Prudery and Passion: Sexuality in Victorian America.* New York, 1971.

Rutherford, Mildred. *American Literature.* Atlanta, 1902.

Sennett, Richard. *Families Against the City: Middle Class Homes of Industrial Chicago, 1872–1890.* Cambridge, 1970.

Shackleton, Robert. *The Book of Chicago.* Philadelphia, 1920.

Stead, William T. *If Christ Came to Chicago.* New York, 1964 reprint.

Stone, Herbert S. *First Editions of American Authors.* Cambridge, 1893.

Stone, Melville E. *Fifty Years a Journalist.* New York, 1921.

Taylor, Graham. *Chicago Commons Through Forty Years.* Chicago, 1936.

Thompson, Slason. *Eugene Field: A Study in Heredity and Contradictions.* 2 vols. New York, 1901.

————. *Life of Eugene Field: The Poet of Childhood.* New York and London, 1927.

Westlake, J. Willis. *Common School Literature.* Philadelphia, 1898.

Wilson, Francis. *The Eugene Field I Knew.* New York, 1898.

————. *Francis Wilson's Life of Himself.* Boston and New York, 1924.

Wilson, Harold S. *McClure's Magazine and the Muckrakers.* Princeton, 1970.

Wilson, Rufus R. *New England in Letters.* New York, 1904.

Young, Art. *On My Way: Being the Book of Art Young in Text and Picture.* New York, 1928.

Young, Ella Flagg. *The Young and Field Literary Reader.* Boston, 1914.

Ziff, Larzer. *The American 1890's: Life and Times of a Lost Generation.* New York, 1966.

ARTICLES

Brown, Joseph G. "My Recollections of Eugene Field as a Journalist in Denver," *Colorado Magazine,* **4** (1927), 41–49.

Burke, H. R. "Eugene Field's Newspaper Days in St. Louis," *Missouri Historical Review,* **41** (1947), 137–146.

Day, Robert A. "The Birth and Death of a Satirist," *American Literature,* **22** (1951), 466–478.

Debs, E. V. "Recollections of Riley, Nye and Field," *National Magazine,* **39** (1914), 611–617.

Flanagan, J. T. "Eugene Field after Sixty Years," *University of Kansas City Review,* **13** (1945), 167–173.

Goodrich, Mary. "The Vogue in Revival," *Overland Monthly,* **87** (1929), 271–272.

Hoffman, F. S. "Eugene Field as I Knew Him at Knox," *The Knox Alumnus* (1924), 89–92.

Kelsoe, W. A. "Eugene Field's St. Louis Newspaper Work," *Missouri Historical Review,* **27** (1932), 78–79.

Larned, W. T. "The Mantle of Eugene Field," *Bookman,* **41** (1915), 44–57.

Monroe, Harriet. "An Unpublished Letter from Eugene Field," *Poetry,* **28** (1926), 268–274.

Morse, Willard. "Check List Books By and About Eugene Field," unpublished (1926).

Parsons, Eugene. "Eugene Field in Denver," *Bellman,* **26** (1919), 123–125.

Reedy, William M. "The Eugene Field Myth," *The Mirror Pamphlets,* **3** (1901), 1–19.

Stewart, Walter. "Eugene Field: Pioneer 'Colyumist,' Managing Editor, and Poet," *Journalism Quarterly*, **43** (1966), 57–66.

Ticknor, Caroline. "Edmund Clarence Stedman and Eugene Field," *Bookman*, **27** (1908), 147–151.

———. "Eugene Field and His First Publisher," *Bookman*, **39** (1914), 514–526.

Valentine, John. "Collector's Field," *Publishers Weekly*, **148** (1945), 223–225.

Weill, E. E. "Eugene Field," *McBride's*, **96** (1915), 109–116.

Wilson, Francis. "Eugene Field, The Humorist," *Century*, **64** (1902), 446–452.

Index

FINIS

Typographical note:

Text Type: 12/15 pt. Scotch
Chapter Headings: 30 pt. Bocklin

❧❧